For Freedom and Prosperity:

Philip M. McKenna and the Gold Standard League

For Freedom and Prosperity:

Philip M. McKenna and the Gold Standard League

by

Gary M. Quinlivan, PhD
and
Brian Surkan

foreword by

T. William Boxx

CENTER FOR ECONOMIC AND POLICY EDUCATION AND THE SAINT VINCENT COLLEGE CENTER FOR NORTHERN APPALACHIAN STUDIES

Saint Vincent College, 300 Fraser Purchase Rd., Latrobe PA 15650

Printed in the United States of America
Cover design by J.S. Downs and Associates

Library of Congress Cataloging-in-Publication Data

Quinlivan, Gary M., 1952-
For freedom and prosperity: Philip M. McKenna and the Gold Standard League / by Gary Quinlivan and Brian Surkan: with a foreword by T. William Boxx.
p. cm.
Includes bibliographical references and index.
ISBN 1-885851-14-6
1. Money—United States—History. 2. Gold standard —History. 3. Monetary policy—United States—History. 4. McKenna, Philip M. (Philip Mowry). 1897-1969. 5. Gold Standard League—History.
I. Surkan, Brian, 1973- . II. Title.
HG501.Q56 1999 99-25096
332.4 973-dc21 CIP

In Memoriam
Philip M. McKenna

Contents

Acknowledgments

Our strongest appreciation goes to T. William Boxx, the Chairman and CEO of the Philip M. McKenna Foundation, for providing us access to the thousands of pages of letters authored by the inventor, entrepreneur, and scholar, Philip M. McKenna. In addition, we thank Bill for providing us with the inspiration to finish this book and also for the insightful essay he authored, which is the foreword of our book.

If he were still alive, we would thank Philip M. McKenna, the founder of Kennametal Inc. and a renaissance man. He not only believed that the values and attributes, which constitute a healthy society, require free markets unimpeded by government intervention, he took action and devoted a large share of his life in defense of those principles.

The authors wish to thank Barbara Pestritto who organized the McKenna letters and provided us with valuable comments. We also wish to thank Sandra Quinlivan who carefully proofed our earlier drafts and strongly affected the method in which we presented McKenna's monetary philosophy. Sandra Quinlivan and Pilar Herr are currently typing all McKenna authored letters. The Center for Economic and Policy Education plans to make these letters available on disk to the general public in the near future. Sandra Quinlivan also provided us with the index for this book.

A special thanks to Anthony Pitts, one of Quinlivan's teaching assistants at Carnegie Mellon University (1998/99) and a Ph.D. candidate in economics at Penn State University and to Richard

Kessler, an economics major at Saint Vincent College. Anthony provided us with valuable data on United States Treasury gold reserve holdings. Richard provided an initial scanning of all our photographs and related materials.

We thank Russell Dickens, C'55 at Saint Vincent College. It was Mr. Dickens who told us that the Bureau of Mint had issued a gold coin to honor F.D. Roosevelt. See Chapter 5.

We express our appreciation to the Saint Vincent College Center for Northern Appalachian Studies and especially Dr. Richard D. Wissolik for co-publishing our book. Wissolik also provided us with several valuable stylistic comments.

Finally, we thank the Philip M. McKenna Foundation for providing the financial support that made this book possible. All photographs and Kennametal Inc. promotional material, appearing in the photo chapter of this book, were provided by the Philip M. McKenna Foundation. We owe a special debt of thanks to Kennametal Inc. for permission to reprint the Kennametal advertisements. The Kennametal advertisements, which appear in the photo section, are representative of Kennametal Inc.'s monetary views during that time period, 1948 to 1950, when the advertisements where published. Philip M. McKenna's and Kennametal Inc.'s monetary and political views, which are expressed in the Kennametal advertisements, were conditioned by the macroeconomic and political events of the 1930s and 1940s.

Gary M. Quinlivan is the Executive Director of the Center for Economic and Policy Education and Chairman of the Economics, Political Science and Public Policy Departments at Saint Vincent College in Latrobe, Pennsylvania. Quinlivan received his Ph.D. in economics at the University at Albany in New York.

Brian Surkan is a monetary economist living and writing in Boston. Surkan has a B.S. in computer science and economics from Carnegie Mellon University.

Foreword

The cover story of the September 20, 1952 *Business Week* featured Philip M. McKenna and the company he founded and ran —Kennametal Inc. The focus of the article was Kennametal's efforts to develop a jet engine formed from titanium carbide that could withstand the higher temperatures needed for greater power performance. But as the reporter soon discovered, one could not long speak with Philip McKenna without being engaged on the subject of political economics in general and the gold standard in particular. As the article says, "although it is oversimplifying somewhat to say it, McKenna's entire non-metallurgical existence is bound-up in reestablishing the gold standard . . ." Philip believed that a gold-based monetary policy required the government to be financially responsible, which meant lower taxes and thus more money for individuals and businesses. The result would be greater economic stability, growth and entrepreneurial development.

With a far reaching mind and in many ways ahead of his time, Philip was both an intellectual and a man of action, which his founding of the Gold Standard League in 1949 demonstrates. This was a relatively new kind of organization that combined credible intellectual argumentation in the public arena with policy advocacy. In this sense, it anticipated the later "think tank" movement, which would take off in the 1970s and 1980s in response to the growth of government. Scholarly and forward looking, he recognized the power of ideas and good scholarship, perhaps best exemplified by his financial support of the English translation of Ludwig von Mises' *The Theory of Money and Credit*, thus introducing this eventually famous work to American audiences.

At the heart of this passionate commitment to sound monetary policy was Philip's firm belief that America's freedom as well as the necessary conditions for prosperity were at stake. Socialism and communism were on the rise, internationally and domestically, and Philip saw the abandonment of the gold standard, which had been an inherent limitation on the power of government, as a step toward these misguided and ruinous philosophies. He realized that America's economic strength was "nurtured on Constitutional freedom." Combined with those political principles was a strong appreciation for the moral-cultural tradition of America and the West.

In a letter to Professor Walter Lichtenstein of Harvard University, he wrote:

> I believe Americans are capable of raising up a standard which will build up a system based upon the Judeo-Christian ethic that the individual human being is the building block which is worthy of protection as a creature of God, while man-made entities such as governments based on power alone, monopolies in banking, in labor monopolies and other organized aggressions are merely products of weak and fallible men and thus may and should be dissolved or decentralized.

In this, one is struck by his foreshadowing of the contemporary movement to decentralize or devolve governmental power as well as the similarity to later political theologians such as Michael Novak who would base economic freedom in Man's dignity as creatures of the Creator.

Philip had a spiritual-based personal philosophy and a strong sense of providence working in his life. He ascribed his and his father's success to "a sense of abstract and spiritual values." Man was in the world "[a]s an exemplification of the Will that rules everything." Human thinking and action should follow "the Will, or God's purpose." He felt that his own research and vocational focus had a providential aspect in regards to preparing for World War I:

> Because I was working in the refining of tungsten in 1914 then, as now, a factor in war strength in a struggle for greater output of material, I felt I was, in a certain field, actually a part of one of God's tools, carrying out a principle to be demonstrated. It seemed providential that before the World War I had started I had been engaged in [this] project. . . .

This sense of providence was coupled with a natural law philosophy not unlike America's Founding Fathers. He believed in "[t]he world God made with laws one could discover." Philosophically describing his life he said: "I followed the hard path which God had cut out for me by revelation of some of the smaller laws I was possessed to follow."

He had a keen appreciation for the study of history and Man's role in discovering the work of providence in it:

> A feeling of awe and respect for history, which has been described as 'God working by experiment' has been with me ever since I can remember. Trying to comprehend, even dimly, the Principles which God establishes or uses, as a workman uses tools, may be considered by some as presumptuous or even blasphemous, but I do not hold it so. . . . To the religious philosopher I suppose this thought may be better expressed by saying our minds are more or less imperfect parts of God's mind.

Philip was, above all, a man of principle who was motivated to public action by his apprehension of the threats to America's freedom, prosperity, and good order. His personal and public philosophies were ultimately rooted in a sense of divine providence and natural law, much like the American founders. He was a patriotic citizen who believed passionately in the free society, exemplified by free enterprise, limited constitutional government, and Judeo-Christian tradition.

On behalf of the Philip M. McKenna Foundation and Philip's intellectual legacy, I am happy to commend this monograph in recognition of the thirtieth anniversary of Philip's death.

T. William Boxx
Chairman
Philip M. McKenna Foundation, Inc.
January 1999

1

Introduction

"Human liberty rests on gold redeemable money."[1]

In 1949, fearing disintegrating economic stability in the United States, Philip M. McKenna founded the Gold Standard League to push for a nationwide return to the gold standard. Restoration of the gold standard was a very serious issue for Philip McKenna to which he devoted several years of his life. As National Chairman (1949 to 1955) of the Gold Standard League, he wrote prolifically to politicians and influential people, gave lectures, published articles, conducted conferences, and distributed publications. He functioned as both a public policy advocate, promoting legislation to restore the gold standard, and as an educator, convincing the general public and opinion leaders of the efficacy of a gold-based monetary system.

McKenna likened the gold standard in society to a fuse in an electrical system: it unobtrusively facilitates normal activities, providing a regulatory safeguard to protect the system from anomalies. To abandon such a standard would be tantamount to replacing the fuse with a copper penny.

According to McKenna, many of society's ills, including

---

[1] Philip M. McKenna, Founder and National Chairman of the Gold Standard League. McKenna was the founder and former CEO of Kennametal Inc. McKenna's biography is presented in the Appendix, pages 55–58.

socialized medicine, inflation and unemployment could be avoided by simply returning to a gold standard. He also believed that economic systems could have a positive or negative effect on the moral life of society. In a paper he wrote entitled, "The Gold Standard and Public Morals," McKenna blamed England's and France's socialistic systems for contributing to an increase in gambling, lack of thrift, and excessive personal spending on luxury goods. He supported the gold standard, not only because he thought it the best way to control inflation and promote prosperity, but also because: "It is the best practical unit of value for a country based upon biblical principles and a constitution designed to protect the individual from the monsters of man's creation."[2]

McKenna specifically favored a redeemable gold coin standard, whereby paper dollars can be redeemed *on demand* for gold dollar coins. A non-convertible system (e.g., the United States' domestic monetary system from 1934 to 1971) would have allowed the monetary authority the flexibility to change the ratio between the money supply (checkable deposits plus currency and coin in circulation) and the amount of specie held in reserve. As a consequence, the monetary authority would have the power to print money.[3]

McKenna's virulent distaste for fiat currency is rooted in his objection to indirect taxation. With direct taxation, elected representatives must vote on the amount of, and details of, any new tax, and the tax appears in the budget. With indirect taxation, taxes

---

[2] Letter to Dr. Edwin G. Nourse (Chair of the Council of Economic Advisors from 1946 to 1949) April 13, 1950.

[3] From 1933 to 1958, the gold reserve ratio was 40 percent for notes and 35 percent for deposits. Due to large gold outflows, in 1958 "the law was changed to require a uniform 25 percent [gold reserve ratio on currency and deposits]" (Milton Friedman and Anna J. Schwartz, *A Monetary History of the United States, 1867–1960*, Princeton University Press, Princeton, 1963, p. 471).

are not explicitly levied, but collected by printing money which in turn artificially raises the prices of goods and services. McKenna supported the gold coin standard because it was *less* susceptible to indirect taxation.

His convictions about the gold standard originated in the 1920s but were intensified when FDR issued an executive order, on April 5, 1933, prohibiting the private ownership of gold.[4] McKenna published his first article about the gold standard in 1943, when America was still under a quasi-gold standard (Bretton Woods), a time when most people had either lived under a redeemable gold coin standard, or heard of it from their parents. McKenna was not alone in his quest. His supporters included numerous bankers, politicians, economists, and businessmen.

Most contemporary Americans have never known a redeemable gold standard or any other specie currency. To such ears, McKenna's strong sentiments may ring of irrational radicalism. But not everyone has shunned the role of gold in monetary policy. Wayne Angell, Alan Greenspan, and other economists have recently suggested either targeting the price of gold in dollars or at least closely monitoring the price as a harbinger of inflation.[5] Before passing judgement, we must take into account the historical framework which conditioned McKenna's opinions. Given McKenna's time frame, even Alan Greenspan had strongly shared McKenna's convictions about gold. In an essay written in 1962 on "Gold and Economic Freedom," Greenspan goes so far as to declare

---

[4] Milton Friedman and Anna J. Schwartz, *A Monetary History of the United States, 1867–1960*, Princeton University Press, Princeton, 1963, pp. 462–464.

[5] See Walsh, Carl E., "A Primer on Monetary Policy Part II: Targets and Indicators," *FRBSF Weekly Letter*, Number 94-28, August 19, 1994, p. 3. See Wayne Angell, "The Fed: On the Right Course," *Wall Street Journal*, December 16, 1997, p. A18. Also, "Time to Relax, Alan," *Wall Street Journal*, August 31, 1998, p. 18.

> . . . that gold and economic freedom are inseparable, that the gold standard is an instrument of laissez-faire [markets] and that each implies and requires the other. . . .
>
> In the absence of the gold standard, there is no way to protect savings from confiscation through inflation. There is no safe store of value. If there were the government would have to make its holdings illegal, as was done in the case of gold.[6]

Other economists and financial pundits have suggested a role for gold (or the United States dollar) as a reserve currency to restore confidence in the Russian ruble, to establish a single currency for Southeast Asia, and to anchor the purchasing power of the currencies of developing countries that are prone to high inflation rates.

McKenna's logic was sound both in the context of his era and that of currently accepted economic fundamentals. He strongly believed that the monetary honesty imposed by an unencumbered gold standard results in an inherently stable economy. McKenna would have his share of supporters today. From Milton Friedman and Bennett McCallum, who favor monetary rules over the discretion of the Federal Reserve Open Market Committee, to Wayne Angell, who would like to see a more prominent role for gold in terms of money supply growth.[7] Supporters of currency boards have suggested monetary systems, for inflation plagued countries, based on the convertibility of gold reserves.[8]

---

[6] *Capitalism: The Unknown Ideal*, edited by Ayn Rand, Penguin Group, NY, NY, the copyright of Greenspan's article is 1962, p. 96.

[7] Mishkin, Frederic S., *The Economics of Money, Banking, and Financial Markets*, Addison Wesley Longman, Inc., Reading, Massachusetts, 1998, pp. 544–548 and 679–684. Also, McCallum, Bennett T., *Monetary Economics: Theory and Policy*, Macmillan Publishing Company, New York, 1989, ch. 12 and 16.

[8] See Hanke, Steve, Jonung, Lars, and Schuler, Kurt, *Russian Currency and Finance: a currency board approach to reform*, Routledge, New York, 1993, p. 101. Also see Shelton, Judy, "Russia Need a New Currency . . .," *Wall Street Journal*,

This treatise provides a history of the Gold Standard League and the philosophical pro-gold arguments of inventor and industrialist, Philip M. McKenna. The book begins with an article McKenna published in the *Commercial and Financial Chronicle*. It was this article that identified his gold standard beliefs. We then present his first public lecture, which provided McKenna the motivation to found the Gold Standard League. The rest of this manuscript is devoted to McKenna's founding of and work associated with the Gold Standard League; his strong belief in the gold standard's power to preserve human liberty, democracy, and economic strength; a critique of President Franklin Delano Roosevelt's economic policies; his distrust of government motivations; and his views on gold as a standard of value. The appendix contains a biography of Philip M. McKenna, a listing of the Gold Standard League members, and Congressional Bills: HR 5031 and HR 3262. The photo section, which follows the appendix, contains letters of correspondence with Ludwig von Mises, several pictures of individuals who were involved in McKenna's gold standard endeavors, Kennametal Inc.'s pro-gold standard advertisement bulletins, Gold Standard Leaque literature written by Philip. M. McKenna, a picture of Alex G. McKenna (Philip's first cousin and former President and CEO of Kennametal Inc.) and Donald C. McKenna (Philip's brother and Chairman of the Board of Kennametal Inc.), and a few assorted random pictures.

August 20, 1998, p. A14.

2

McKenna's Enlightenment: The Importance of Sound, Redeemable Money

On May 27, 1943 the *Commercial and Financial Chronicle* published McKenna's first essay on money, clearly delineating his reasons for believing that sound, redeemable money plays an essential role in the preservation of freedom. It also details desirable properties of money as a medium of exchange, a unit of account and as a standard of value. It further underlines the importance of having markets that are free of government manipulation. McKenna later wrote that this essay was his first act upon "waking up" to the full implications of America's abandonment of the gold standard.

"Money is a Tool"

Money is a tool which mankind has found useful. Without this invention of a common denominator by which evaluation of alternate courses of action can be accomplished, mankind is without a guiding compass. The industrialist asks, for instance, should I replace one process of manufacture by another method, and calls on the cost engineer to make an equation. Into this equation go the hours of work of persons at the varying rates of pay to which their skill, training and other considerations entitle them; the amounts of materials, electricity instead of gas for instance, or a larger weight of cast iron for a smaller weight of higher priced steel; and the labor and skill required to make the changes. The farmer asks does it pay to grow corn on this field and feed it to hogs, or should I grow wheat and sell it for making flour. The politician is not aware of the nicety and accuracy of these computations required for wise conduct of business, industry and agriculture, and how distortion of the measuring tool, money, may lose our country actual man hours and physical goods. To destroy a large animal it is only necessary to strike certain brain centers with a bullet, and the animal dies because its faculty of coordination is destroyed. Similarly, when an important economic principle, normally guiding and coordinating the activity of a nation is destroyed, the nation is apt to be rendered impotent and unable to defend itself. 'Whom the Gods would destroy they first make mad.'

When the normal functions of money are inhibited by laws and restraints are put upon the use of money for facilitating exchanges of goods and services, the country as a whole loses efficiency, because a clumsy barter method or the like must be employed instead. By doing away with money, in whole or in part, we do not alter the underlying motivation of the individual which is the possibility of gain. Exchange simply takes another and often wasteful form. For example, since monetary profit in war industry is frowned upon, means are found to induce corporation managers to expand facilities with government money, with the unstated but real motivation that they shall have control of the acquired machinery and plant after the war. Log-rolling of all sorts takes place. Instead of having to produce only the goods necessary to fight the war an equal amount of goods in value must also be ordered and producers induced to accept [the goods] in lieu of monetary profits and additional facilities they [would have] acquire[d] . . . Small wonder that our living standards are lowered, because of the inefficiency of motivation by barter.

This assault upon freedom of use of money as a standard began when we technically abandoned the gold standard about 1933. It came to my attention in 1942, by the proposals to seize from the 'haves' not only money but also patents, and other property, that the 'revolutionists' had become aware of that inequality prevailed not only in differences in the amount of money possessed by individuals, but inasmuch as ideas are definitely intangible property, they sought to seize the only tangible and visible form of this property that they could see, namely the printed patent paper. . . . for the benefit of the 'have-nots.'

It is not realized that the well-being of the 'have-nots' would be more rapidly and more surely improved by the normal effect of the competitive system. Those favoring such seizures remind me of the half grown chickens to whom I fed sour milk in a large pan; in their haste to get at it they get into the pan and waste this valuable food by splattering. An orderly method of feeding them was necessary to avoid loss and provide for the general welfare of all.

Therefore, . . . I should say that whether we can support a $300 billion debt, or any debt, is dependent upon whether we are to have restored to us a sound currency, upon which all present and future commitments in business can be reasonably and fairly based, and whether invention and technical progress will be protected by law as guaranteed by the Constitution or destroyed by attempts to hamper and shackle those having special knowledge and the will to improve our common lot.

McKenna was determined to inform others about the government's "assault" on the freedom of the American people. As part of his continuing efforts to broaden awareness of the issue of sound money, McKenna addressed the Latrobe Rotary Club in August, 1948. The response to his talk, his first public speaking engagement addressing the issue of the gold standard, was enthusiastic and the lecture was printed in local papers.

He begins by correctly correlating the printing of money to a loss of purchasing power and a decline in real asset values when investments have a fixed stream of payments.

. . . It [money] is a measuring tool for use in daily transactions and for measuring fair value; also in transaction of business over a period of time. How well it serves the purpose of honest men depends upon the degree of certainty which they may place upon its present and future value.

. . . it is hard to tell you the losses suffered by the thrifty and frugal people of America who have seen their dollar savings more than cut in two in purchasing power. The orphan, the widow and the old retired folks suffer silently without making any fuss. Every dollar of savings in the form of savings bank accounts, life insurance, preferred stocks and bonds is now buying less than half of what it did when it was saved ten years ago. A deteriorating currency robs all who work and save. Economists soberly estimate that the dollar will continue to depreciate about 3 percent a year in the foreseeable future unless a great change comes in our country's monetary policy.[9] This year I should guess the deterioration to have been greater than this, as much as 10 per cent in

---

[9]Inflation rates averaged 3.9 percent per year from December 1948 to June 1998. Data is from the Bureau of Labor Statistics website http://stats.bls.gov/top20.

> a single year.[10] Is there no hope then to attain a non-deteriorating money in America?
>
> . . . The remedy is needed now. One does not have to be an expert or a prophet to see the eventual disaster if this money deterioration continues. . . . Our real salvation lies in restoring promptly to the American people the use of sound money by which the wage earner and his savings are protected as well as the honest investor of larger amounts.

McKenna tells his audience that he prefers a gold standard with a redeemable currency. He also asserts that there is a connection between money being redeemable in gold and human liberty—the nationalization of gold, he claims, lessens personal freedom and is the tool of totalitarian governments to overturn "the existing social order."

> At this point you may wish to know precisely what I mean by sound money as distinguished from irredeemable pieces of paper. I mean a medium of exchange which within itself possesses a given quantity of a thing of intrinsic value or at the option of the owner is convertible into a specified quantity of a thing of intrinsic value. As an example, a gold coin of a given standard of weight and fineness is a medium of exchange possessing intrinsic value. Come war or revolution or repudiation, coins minted from gold or any other metal possess the value of their metallic content. I am sorry I haven't a $20 gold piece to show you, because in 1934 a tyrannical law was enacted which required all gold coins to be turned into the Treasury in return for which the owner was given $20 per ounce in irredeemable paper money; and shortly thereafter the government declared gold to be worth $35 an ounce instead of $20.67 an ounce as was standard before 1933.
>
> When you recall that one of the first moves by Lenin, Mussolini and Hitler was to outlaw individual ownership of gold, you begin to sense that there may be some connection between money, redeemable in gold, and the rare prize known as human liberty.
>
> . . . Also when you find that Lenin declared and demonstrated that a sure way to overturn the existing social order was by printing press

---

[10] Inflation in 1948 was 8.1 percent. Data is from the Bureau of Labor Statistics website http://stats.bls.gov/top20.

> paper money, then again you are impressed with the possibility of a relationship between a gold backed money and human freedom.
> . . .

McKenna goes on to note that inflation causes economic chaos by sending out incorrect market signals. According to McKenna, "money illusion" blinds people to the impending loss of purchasing power caused by printing money and it only gets worse—once the economic turmoil becomes apparent, governments have a tendency to impose even more market distortions, such as "price-fixing, wage-fixing and rationing."[11]

> . . . When, in all history, did irredeemable paper money controlled by politicians ever follow any other path than deterioration followed by disorders caused by financial uncertainty and robbery of the thrifty and capable. I have no time to portray the end of the road of all paper money experiments. It is worse than just high prices. Monetary chaos was followed in the French Revolution by the tyranny of Napoleon not broken until 1815 after 25 years of suffering and war by the common citizen in France; in Germany inflation was followed by Hitler; in Russia by Bolshevism; and in other nations by more or less tyranny. Suppose the frugal savings of the humble people of America continue to deteriorate in the next 10 years as they have in the past 10 years. Some day the people will almost certainly flock to 'a man on horseback' who says he will stop 'inflation' by price-fixing, wage-fixing and rationing. When currency loses its exchange value the processes of production and distribution are demoralized.

But there was still time for economic salvation, McKenna advised his listeners to actively support Representative Howard

---

[11] In response to inflation passing 4 percent annual rate in the early 70s, Nixon imposed wage and price controls, but as noted by Samuelson and Nordhaus, the controls "appear to have been totally ineffective . . ." The price and wage controls proved easy to evade. See Samuelson, Paul A. and Nordhaus, William D., *Economics*, Fifteenth Edition, McGraw-Hill, Inc., co. 1995, p. 596.

Buffet's bill, HR 5031, which would return the United States to the gold standard.[12]

> Fortunately if citizens are awake and know the facts as to the need for speedy return to a gold coin standard in the USA, we have an effective remedy. It depends upon your promptly writing to your Congressman and talking with your representatives in political life telling them to enact House of Representatives Bill HR 5031 introduced Jan. 20, 1948 entitled 'A Bill, to restore the right of American citizens to freely own gold and gold coins; to return control over the public purse to the people; to refrain further deterioration of our currency; to enable holders of paper money to redeem it in gold coin on demand; to establish and maintain a domestic gold coin standard and for other purposes.'
>
> This bill introduced by Representative Howard Buffet of Nebraska has been receiving the enthusiastic support of honest men all over our country. . . . I have many startling and true studies showing the urgent need and also the immediate practicability of this bill. We have the gold in the Treasury now—Twenty-three billions of dollars [of gold].
>
> In the words of Representative Buffett, 'unless you are willing to surrender your children and your country to galloping inflation, war and slavery, then this cause demands your support. For if human liberty is to survive in America we must win the battle to restore honest money. There is no more important challenge facing us than this issue—the restoration of your freedom to exchange gold for the fruits of your labors.'
>
> . . .
>
> If Buffett's bill is enacted, I see there can be a long time of great confidence and prosperity for us and all America. If it is not and we don't return to sound money, I am sure there will be more government, trouble, waste, disorder, distrust and eventual war and slavery.
>
> But we've got to do something to overcome the apathy of the citizens about this. Every wise and honest man will help.
>
> . . .

The themes of this speech would be heard again and again as McKenna gave similar presentations across Pennsylvania and,

---

[12] See photo 3 for a picture of Representative Howard Buffett (Warren's father). The entirety of HR 5031 is reproduced in the Appendix, pp. 60–62.

eventually, throughout the country. McKenna found that other citizens were as concerned about the issue of sound money as he was, and, in June of 1949, he started the Gold Standard League in order to facilitate communication among individuals around the country who shared his beliefs on this issue.

ERRATUM

Page 19, Note 21

The note should read:

Philip's time commitment to the Gold Standard League did not hinder the day to day operations of Kennametal Inc. because the company had a strong management team ably led by his cousin and founding General Partner, Alex G. McKenna, who was Executive Vice President and the chief operating officer, along with the advice and assistance of Donald C. McKenna, Philip's brother, who was a key member of the Board and a founding partner. Alex and Donald would later become President and CEO and Chairman of the Board, respectively.

3

The Gold Standard League

The Gold Standard League's declared purpose was "to provide for research, publication, and dissemination of information on all subjects involved in [the] science of sound monetary economics and more particularly to encourage discussions of a gold coin standard—$35 per ounce—as means of giving our people the best type of money system and of restoring to our people control over their public purse."[13] Far from radical when it was formed in 1949, the League appealed to many Americans who had lived under the Gold Standard and were aware of the long-term stability in prices associated with commodity standards–from 1800 to 1933, CPI measured prices decreased 19.8 percent.[14] Without the natural

---

[13] This is the mission statement on the letterhead of the Gold Standard League.

[14] Although the decline was not monotonic. From 1800 to 1860, the consumer price index declined 47 percent. During the Civil War, the United States dropped off the gold standard in 1862 and prices rose 70.3 percent from 1860 to 1865. Prices dropped 45.7 percent over the next 35 years primarily because the United States resumed gold payments in 1879 at pre-Civil war gold-dollar conversion rates. From 1900 to 1920, prices increased 240 percent and then declined 31.8 percent between 1920 and 1933 (See McCallum, Bennett T., *Monetary Economics, Theory and Policy*, Macmillan Publishing Company, New York, 1989, p. 4, Table 1-1). Prior to 1900, the United States had a bimetallic standard. Between 1900 and 1933, domestic residents could exchange dollars for gold at an exchange rate of $20.67 to one ounce of gold. As noted by Bennett T. McCallum, pp. 329–330, the abandonment of the gold standard is not clearly dated. The United States nationalized the gold market in 1933 and forbid private ownership. Gold and gold coins were called in April 5, 1933 (Milton Friedman and Anna J. Schwartz, *A Monetary History of the United States, 1867–1960*,

monetary constraints imposed by the gold standard, the federal government, McKenna predicted, would avail itself of the ability to inflate the currency. McKenna's dire prediction proved accurate—from December 1933 to June 1998, CPI measured prices increased by 1,134.8 percent.[15]

As the National Chairman of the Gold Standard League, McKenna attempted to persuade politicians, business leaders and private citizens that America's abandonment of the gold standard was a threat to their freedom. He believed that the apathy he constantly encountered when speaking about the gold standard was due to people's failure to understand the connection between their freedom and redeemable money.

Irredeemable currency usurped people's freedom because it allowed the government to print money to finance debt without the approval of citizens. As the Gold Standard League explained in its bulletin of April 7, 1951, the "gold standard permits government to go into debt for purposes of which people approve and for which they agree to taxation to liquidate in the long run and for which they will buy bonds." Without the gold standard, the approval of the people is not necessary.

In September, 1949, McKenna attended the International Gold

Princeton University Press, Princeton, 1963, pp. 462–464). However, it was not until August of 1971 that Nixon closed the gold window to foreign central banks—ending the Bretton Woods fixed exchange rate system. Also see footnote 48 in this book.

[15] Updated CPI figures were obtained from the Bureau of Labor Statistics at their website, http://stats.bls.gov/. According to Michael F. Bryan, the assistant vice president and economist at the Federal Reserve Bank of Cleveland, "If the United States had been on a gold standard between 1973 and 1996, we would likely have experienced no inflation . . . since the price of gold relative to the CPI is nearly the same today as it was 24 years ago" (Bryan, Michael F., "Bad Standards," *Economic Commentary*, Federal Reserve Bank of Cleveland, October 1, 1997). On the downside, Bryan believes that prices may have been more volatile during this time period due to the volatility of the market price of gold. But Bryan also notes (footnote 4) that "some of this volatility would have been reduced had there been a more stable price level over the period."

Coin Conference in New York City, where he gave a speech entitled, "How to Return to the Gold Standard Now."[16] McKenna outlines the reasons why the Gold Standard League was founded, as well as the manner in which this was accomplished.

> How can American citizens get back that necessary implement of human liberty, redeemable money? Several years ago I listened to a speech tracing the evil effects of printing-press money, politically-managed money and credit on the life of our people. The speaker described, as many of us confirm by our studies of the history of irredeemable paper money, the eventual fate of monetary systems in which the currency is not required to be made good in the metal which is our standard of value.
>
> I listened to that speaker and at the end asked timidly, 'But who will put the bell on the cat?' reminding him of the council of mice who decided that the way to stop the depredations of the cat which was devouring them one by one was to require that the cat wear a bell (I propose a golden bell) to give due notice of the cat's approach. Of course, one way to bring the cat to its senses is to let it devour most of the mice, until it commences to starve because of their *extinguishment*. But that method is so unnecessarily painful to the citizens! It amounts to going through a political revolution such as we have seen in Russia and in England.
>
> As a rather adventurous mouse, I decided that, having a few crumbs of cheese stuck away in the hills of Western Pennsylvania, I'd see what I could do in the way of 'belling the cat' while we still had a limited independence. We started the activities which are now 'The Gold Standard League' a little more than a year ago in Pennsylvania. In June of this year, with State Chairmen in eight states we announced ourselves

---

[16] This speech was sponsored by the Economists' National Committee on Monetary Policy, Hotel Roosevelt, New York City, Sept. 8, 1949. The meeting was attended by 400 business and financial leaders. Plans were set forth to select chairmen for the 48 states and Vice Chairmen for each of the 435 Congressional Districts. Other speakers included: Philip Le Boutillier (President, Best & Co., Inc. NYC), Dr. James Washington Bell (President, Economist's National Committee on Monetary Policy and Chairperson of Economics at Northwestern University), and William W. Cumberland (Partner, Ladenburg, Thalmann & Co.).

> as The Gold Standard League.[17] We had the immense reserve of facts and arguments carefully collected and advanced by the Economists' National Committee on Monetary Policy since their formation in November, 1933, to warn and advise against the actions taken in 1933 and 1934 which took us off the gold standard for use domestically by American citizens.
>
> . . .

McKenna proceeds to describe his serendipitous method of simultaneously advertising both his company's products and the merits of the gold standard.[18] He also talked about the publication of several letters he wrote and the League's public relations efforts.[19]

> Having to write interest-compelling advertisements for our company I realized that I could tell more people quickly if I mentioned the gold standard in our regular trade paper advertising. We got out a series of seven 'ads' entitled for example, 'Soundness Is Essential in Metal Cutting Tools as in Money Tools' and 'Cheap Tools Shackle Industry and Trade.'[20] My associates naturally had a right to question whether the company benefitted by such advertising. The results were most convincing. Within three months they were saying 'At the rate sales are improving since you have begun to neglect your business for this matter of public interest we suggest you neglect it some more and

---

[17] A listing of the officers and State Chairmen is presented in Appendix, p. 59. Photo 4 shows a Gold Standard League meeting. Photos 5 to 7 portray various educational displays created by the Gold Standard League.

[18] In a letter to Philip LeBoutellier, McKenna describes how he would put ". . . gold standard literature in the lobby [Kennametal's] where visitors and salesmen come. Many have volunteered to help re-establish the gold standard who learned of it by this means." (Letter to Philip LeBoutellier, President of Best and Company, Inc., May, 1949)

[19] For Samples of Gold Standard League literature, see photos 23 to 27.

[20] Sample advertisements are shown in the photo section of this book. See photos 8 to 22.

> harder.'[21] I had discovered a force existing in the American people which needed expression.
>
> . . . Financial newspapers such as *The Commercial & Financial Chronicle* and finally the *Wall Street Journal* began to print my articles or excerpts from them. I saw the editor of an American Federation of Labor newspaper, the *Trade Union Courier*,[22] who, recognizing that the wage earner has much at stake in sound money, published a series of three articles by me, pointing out that labor needs the gold coin standard of money. Six hundred newspapers published my article, 'The Investor and Job Maker Dependent on the Gold Coin Standard of Money.' I wrote 400 doctors in our county, pointing out the connection between socialized medicine and irredeemable paper money. . . .
>
> One of the means we are using to tell the facts which Americans must know is to put out a weekly letter, *The Washington Bulletin of the Gold Standard League*. We expect it will soon have over 10,000 subscribers.[23] Articles of a timely nature appear in it written by our Washington writer, Mr. Lawrence McKenna, by members of the Economists' National Committee on Monetary Policy and by others conversant with monetary facts and legislation.

In addition to trade journals and newspapers, Philip had Kennametal publish ads on the gold standard in the *National Review*, founded by Bill Buckley, which was becoming the flagship publication of the conservative movement. He also placed ads in *The Freeman*, the journal of the Foundation for Economic Education. Philip also constantly wrote internal columns and

---

[21] Philip's time commitment to the Gold Standard League did not hinder the day to day operations of Kennametal Inc. because the company was well-managed by his brother Donald, who was the Chairman of the Board, and by his first cousin Alex G. McKenna, who was the President and CEO. Photo number 35 presents a picture of Donald and Alex dated May 1, 1970.

[22] The *Trade Union Courier*'s circulation at that time was approximately 380,000 (mentioned in McKenna's letter to Philip LeBoutellier, president of Best and Company, May, 1949).

[23] By March 1950, the mailing list consisted of 800 weekly newspapers and most of the daily papers published in the United States. At that date, the Gold Standard League had a mailing list of 7,200.

memos to Kennametal employees explaining his business philosophy, political economic views, and commenting on political affairs. He not only sought to shape the "corporate culture" but also help to educate his employees as good citizens based on sound principles.

McKenna expresses the Gold Standard League's support of House Bill, HR 3262, and commits the League to lobbying efforts consistent with those of the Economists' National Committee on Monetary Policy.[24]

> The Gold Standard League may in the future reinforce, from the viewpoint of general citizens, the advice of the members of the Economists' National Committee on Monetary Policy. For example, in May of this year hearings on the McCarron Bill, HR 13, were held by the Senate's Committee on Banking and Currency. Six or seven of the members of the monetary economists arrived in time to be heard in person. Over 50 of them had time to consider and to send their considered statement put in the record opposing the McCarron Bill and recommending instead the House Bill, HR 3262, introduced by the Hon. Daniel E. Reed of New York, the ranking Republican member of the House Committee on Banking and Currency.[25] The Reed Bill will reestablish the thoroughly constituted gold coin standard with all non-gold U.S. currency redeemable for use by American citizens. Now that we have the Gold Standard League, members among the citizens can appear at such hearings and make their voices heard. We can bring with us resolutions by our civic organizations all over the country. We can strengthen the hands of responsible legislators who would restore honest fiscal policies. We can give them intelligent and effective support in each of their districts. Within a year we must have a sufficient number of responsible citizens in each Congressional district who are informed on the need for restoration of honest money and able to voice and write their opinions.
>
> . . .

---

[24] HR 3262 is reproduced in the Appendix, pp. 63–65.

[25] Photo number 28 shows Congressman Reed delivering a lecture for a Gold Standard League convention in Washington. D.C. on May 5, 1952.

His lecture concludes by linking, once again, the prohibition of owning gold to totalitarian and socialistic governments. McKenna is convinced that the gold standard will "provide a victory for free enterprise" and "democracy."

> It is incompatible with the use of the traditional standard of money of the world, gold, that American citizens should be denied the use of the metal which is our standard of value. On the present limited gold bullion standard, a dollar is nothing more nor less than 1/35th of an ounce of gold. Obligations of the U.S. Treasury are made good in that standard to foreigners, through their foreign central banks, but not to Americans, who are prohibited, by laws which we would repeal, from owning our own standard of value. It places American citizens in a strange category indeed when you consider that the countries prohibiting their people from owning gold or gold coins are Soviet Russia, Socialistic England, and recently Rumania. Among the recent acts of communistic China was to declare the severe penalty of death for anyone having silver or silver dollars. Communistic dictators well know that without money of intrinsic value circulating, the daily lives of the people can be controlled.
>
> The gold coin standard in America provides a victory for free enterprise and represents an example that will be gladly followed in many countries. It is a bloodless way of proving the democratic way of life, with private enterprise, is preferable to the results in the regimented forms of government.
>
> . . .

In a letter (April, 1949) written to E.S. Pillsbury, President of Century Electric Company, McKenna explains his view of the best way to return to the gold standard. In this letter, McKenna argues that, in 1949, there was an unnecessary restriction on credit because the public was worried about long-term inflation. Long-term loans at that time were fixed interest rate loans. As a consequence, banks would have been reluctant to make low interest long-term loans and, to the extent that loans were made, interest rates would have increased by the amount of inflationary expectations. McKenna also argues that the Treasury's gold holdings were large enough to create the additional credit necessary to promote a healthy economy. The

Fed in essence would have the ability to augment the excess reserves of depository institutions to create loans with negligible inflationary consequences.[26] If dollars were once again redeemable into gold, the dollar's value would rise and the Federal Reserve could supply more credit, limited by the amount of gold the Treasury held, without inflation.

McKenna addresses fears that the Bretton Woods System's gold standard would cause gold to flow from the United States to the foreign countries with whom we have balance of payments deficits. He claims that American productivity renders our exports highly desirable to foreigners. We would thus have a tendency to have current account surpluses with corresponding gold inflows. According to Daniel T. Griswold, David Hume would be in full agreement with McKenna: "Hume reasoned that a nation's supply of gold was ultimately determined by its capacity to produce wealth, not the other way around."[27] A more enlightening view, which is derived from Hume's "Specie-Flow Mechanism," is that the resulting gold flows, due to imbalances between the current account and the nonofficial capital account, would cause the appropriate monetary and resulting price level changes to keep the balance of payments of all participating countries near zero. Although unforeseen by McKenna, but predictable given his logic,

---

[26] President James Madison (1809 to 1817) posed a similar argument in 1791, "originally published . . . December 19 and 22, 1791, issues of Philip Freneau's *National Gazette* of Phildelphia" (Madison, James, "Money," essay republished in *Economic Review*, Federal Reserve Bank of Cleveland, 1998, pp. 2–6). President Madison believed that printing money is noninflationary provided it is redeemable into specie at some promised date. The value of money is anchored to gold and is determined by the credibility of the central bank. In 1879, Madison's hypothesis was supported, greenbacks printed to finance the Civil War were made fully convertible to gold at pre-civil war prices, which caused commodity prices to deflate to pre-civil war levels. Also, see Smith, Bruce D., "James Madison's Monetary Economics," *Economic Review*, Federal Reserve Bank of Cleveland, 1998, pp. 7–20.

[27] Griswold, T. Daniel, "America's Maligned and Misunderstood Deficit," *Trade Policy Analysis*, CATO Institute, April 24, 1998, p. 4.

the downfall of Bretton Woods was due to the ability (through control of their printing presses) of central banks to sterilize the equilibriating monetary effects of gold movements. As we approached 1971, exchange rates became severely misaligned causing balance of payments disequilibria to worsen. Eventually the dollar holdings by foreign central banks exceeded the gold stock holdings of the United States Treasury.[28] Speculation then forced the system's collapse and Nixon closed our gold window to foreign central banks in August of 1971.

Finally, McKenna warns, once again, that a failure to return to the gold standard would "push us down into the 'Death Valley' of socialism. . . ." The government had taken over the people's right to own gold and would continue to diminish human liberties to the point of social chaos.

> My conviction is that 'the way to resume is to resume.' I believe that with 12.5 percent gold in the Treasury, compared to the total of all bank credit plus all paper money outstanding now, which compares with only 8.6 percent in 1926 when we were on a redeemable money basis that we have plenty of gold and that resumption wouldn't cause a ripple.[29] In fact, I believe that credit is being constricted for lack of a

---

[28] In 1965, United States gold reserves were surpassed by our dollar liabilities to foreign central banks. By 1972, our gold reserves were valued at approximately $12 billion dollars and our dollar liabilities held by foreign central banks were approximately $60 billion dollars. See Yarbrough, V. Beth and Yarbrough, Robert M., *The World Economy: Trade and Finance*, The Dryden Press Harcourt Brace College Publishers, Fort Worth, 1997, Figure 20.1, p. 840. Also, on the topic of the collapse of the Bretton Woods System, see Kenen, Peter B., *The International Economy*, Third Edition, Cambridge University Press, Cambridge, 1996, pp. 499–501.

[29] McKenna frequently observed that, in 1949, the United States had more gold relative to currency plus all bank deposits than it had prior to 1933 when the currency was redeemable. In 1949, the United States had 24.4 billion dollars worth of monetary gold stock which was 14.5 percent of Friedman and Schwartz's broadest definition of money (i.e., currency held by the public plus demand and time deposits held by commercial banks plus mutual savings bank deposits plus deposits held by the postal savings system). From 1900 to 1932, the

> sound standard, and that conditions are less stable because of the inability of people to make long-term commitments with a feeling of certainty as to the value of money. I believe we shall run into stagnation and inactivity **with** high prices which will be cured only when we resume specie payments. Do we fear drains upon our Treasury because of claims of foreigners who may sell us more goods than we buy? Assuredly not; American productivity has given the dollar great value, causing rather an influx of gold than an outgo in recent years. Now, if ever we can return to redeemable money in the U.S.A., what happens if we don't? Then we **are** indeed gambling, because the public purse is in the hands of political forces which push us down into the 'Death Valley' of socialism, like England. When anyone says to me he regards it as a 'gamble' to return to specie payments now, I tell him that it's the other way, that the 'gamble' is to stay on the present plan of irredeemable paper money which history tells us has never gone any other way than the eventual path of repudiation (and often social chaos and revolution).

In 1962, Alan Greenspan, the current Chairman of the Federal Reserve Bank, likewise drew an unmistakable link between the abolition of the gold standard and socialism.

> . . . The financial policy of the welfare state requires that there be no way for the owners of wealth to protect themselves.
>
> . . .
>
> This is the shabby secret of the welfare statists' tirades against gold. Deficit spending is simply a scheme for the 'hidden' confiscation of wealth. Gold stands in the way of this insidious process. It stands as a

---

ratio of the monetary gold stock to money ranged from a low of 7.2 percent in 1920 to a high of 11.5 percent in 1908. The average of the 33 year gold stock to money ratio from 1900 to 1932 was 9.6 percent. For money supply statistics, see Milton Friedman and Anna J. Schwartz, *A Monetary History of the United States, 1867–1960*, Princeton University Press, Princeton, 1963, Appendix A, Table A-1, pp. 705–719. For Treasury gold stock holdings, see *Historical Statistics of the U.S.: Colonial Times to 1970, Part 2*, United States Department of Commerce, Bureau of the Census, p. 992.

> protector of property rights. If one grasps this, one has no difficulty in understanding the statists' antagonism toward the gold standard.[30]

In May, 1949, McKenna wrote a letter to the president of Best and Company, Inc., Philip LeBoutellier (who later became the League's state chairman in New York), describing the beginnings of the Gold Standard League, their political lobbying efforts, their techniques for informing the public, and ways for others to get involved. Early in his letter, he discusses his concern about "creeping socialism" at universities and his brother's, Donald McKenna, plan to endow a chair in monetary policy to write about gold at Claremont Men's College.[31]

> . . . My brother, Donald C. McKenna, and I had discussed many times in the past three years 'what we must do to be saved'; that is, how to go about restoring our economic freedom to America. Donald thought to do it by education in political economy, which he felt was sadly biased by the lack of real independence of the colleges which were getting a line of C.I.O. and socialistic literature, chiefly from political sources in 'land-grant' colleges. Donald helped found the Claremont Men's College, at Claremont, California, and is now a trustee. They are now founding a chair in monetary policy, looking for a professor who can make speeches and write effectively on behalf of the gold standard.

He explains in this letter how he has successfully involved Kennametal Inc. in his efforts to heighten public awareness of the necessity to return to the gold standard and suggests that businesses should become more involved in supporting the principles in which they believe.

> I wonder why businessmen do not use their advertising to advertise not only their wares, but their principles? Kennametal Inc. has gained much prestige and respect from the better businessmen by this method.

---

[30] *Capitalism: The Unknown Ideal*, edited by Ayn Rand, Penguin Group, NY, NY, the copyright of the Greenspan's article is 1962, p. 96.

[31] Now Claremont McKenna College.

> Tell the public how good your wares are and also how Americans are entitled to use the best kind of money, gold money.
>
> . . .

McKenna goes on to mention his own less than successful effort to have the gold standard adopted into the core of the Republican election campaign.

> . . . I drafted a plank for the Republican Party, which my uncle, a delegate, had introduced, but it was not adopted, except as a very small splinter saying the Republican Party was in favor of 'sound money,' whatever that is.
>
> . . .

Also of interest in the letter was McKenna's outreach to seek the support of the more liberal segments of society—the union and the ministers. In addition to his publications in the A.F.L. paper, the *Trade Union Courier*, McKenna mentions that

> . . . I have a friend in Pittsburgh who volunteers to speak to C.I.O. and A.F.L. meetings on our subject. I have written all ministers in Westmoreland County, quoting Dr. Link's book on *The Gold Standard and Prosperity*.

Finally, McKenna expresses his interest and willingness to serve as the National Chairman of the Gold Standard League.

> I had hoped Mr. B.E. Hutchinson of Chrysler would take on the work of National Chairman of 'The Gold Standard League.' We are fortunate in having Mr. George F. Bauer, who as export manager of the American Auto Manufacturers for some years knows how worthwhile things can be promoted by proper presentation. I shall be very happy to work with the Chairman we select. Lacking anyone else, I shall be ready to undertake it myself, although I should tell you and Mr. Bauer and Dr. Spahr that I am more determined than skillful, more vehement than perhaps effectively persuasive, perhaps imagination and 'will to win' will overcome in part my deficiencies as an organizer; probably Mr. Bauer will be our star organizer. I am a willing worker in Pennsylvania particularly.

This letter is representative of hundreds that McKenna wrote. He was constantly seeking advice, giving advice and soliciting new supporters for his cause. He went to hear and read about speeches given on subjects relating to redeemable money, and he wrote to those who delivered them; he read books and articles on the subject and wrote to the authors; he followed the progress of every bill relating to this subject introduced in Congress, and he wrote to Congressmen and influential business leaders asking them to support such bills. His efforts on behalf of the gold standard were tireless, because he believed American liberty was at stake. His repeated reference to the opinions of dictators and communists on the subject of irredeemable currency demonstrates just how passionately he believed that American democracy would collapse if the gold standard was not restored.

4

Democracy, Economic Strength and Capitalism

McKenna was convinced that the gold standard encouraged democracy, economic strength, and capitalism. In opposition to conventional thought, he asserts that "sound money" is always optimal both in war and in peace. In a letter to George Putnam,[32] he presents Napoleonic France as evidence.

> After the experience of the French Revolutionists and doctrinaires now similarly existing in America toying with the idea of irredeemable paper money, Napoleon said he would return to sound money, and hoped that his enemies would resort to printing press paper money because it would make them so much easier to conquer. Andrew D. White in his book *Fiat Money Inflation in France*, printed in 1896, said Napoleon announced when he took over, 'I will pay cash or I will pay nothing—While I live I will never resort to irredeemable paper money.' He never did and France, according to White 'under this determination, commanded all the gold she needed. When Waterloo came, with the invasion of the Allies, with war on her own soil, with a change of dynasty and with heavy expenses for war and indemnities, France on a specie basis, experienced no financial distress.'

---

[32] August 24, 1950, letter to George Putnam of The George Putnam Fund of Boston. McKenna is responding to a letter Putnam wrote to President Truman. McKenna accuses Putnam of attempting (but unknowingly) to weaken our monetary system, our democracy, and capitalism. McKenna wants Putnam to reverse his opinion and support the passage of Representative Daniel Reed's bill, HR 3262.

A few people with whom McKenna corresponded regarding the gold standard made the objection that the Russians produced gold and America was helping the Russians by buying their gold. In the same letter to George Putnam, McKenna responded to this argument by stating that, "We'd rather have [the Russians] employed mining gold than in making atomic bombs and tanks and marching about in armies threatening the peace of the world. If they settled down to the peaceful production of gold and found that they could buy things with it, the first thing you know they'd turn capitalistic!"

Gold, McKenna goes on to explain, would lead to the downfall of communism:

> Iron curtains may best be penetrated by gold coins. Communistic dictatorship dare not allow individuals the freedom which comes from possession of sound money of universal acceptability. Why not turn Lenin's weapon back upon Russia? If, as he said, the best way to break down a capitalistic society is to debauch the currency by depriving the people of coin of intrinsic value, why isn't the best way to destroy communism to provide the individual Russian or the people of the vast areas which she seeks to control, with the confidence that comes to an individual possessing gold or gold coins. We can do that by buying products and services through individual traders adventurous enough to penetrate the fringe countries around Russia and exchange U.S. gold coins for goods. For instance, tungsten ore in China is undoubtedly difficult for the Communistic government to control. . . . It [tungsten ore] will seep out and gold coins, the thing the Russians cannot tolerate in open circulation will seep in!

McKenna believed that the government's abandonment of the gold standard was only the first step in the erosion of America's freedom. He saw clearly the power gained by the government when currency was no longer redeemable, and he feared that American citizens would continue to surrender more and more of their freedom before they realized what they had done. McKenna's inherent distrust of the government and its motives for taking away redeemable currency is a theme repeated in many of his writings. McKenna argued,

> The small man needs sound money too as well as bankers and foreign central banks. To the latter the Treasury may and does make good in bullion at $35 per ounce. Surely it would be good policy to offer to make good to all American citizens, whose gold it is, whose toil brought it into the Treasury in exchange for our labor and risk-taking, making all non-gold currency redeemable on no other terms than $35 per ounce now available to foreign central banks.[33]

McKenna goes on to describe how a gold standard affects the public's confidence in our financial system, positively affecting real growth domestically and thus invariably augmenting the welfare of the world:

> The productivity of toiling and risk-taking Americans is such that we need have no doubt of our financial resources provided only that the necessary implement of free men, a fixed and sound standard of value be again available to all. It will [intensify] the energies of Americans. It is as necessary in time of war or threats of war, as it is in times of peace. It will revive commerce between citizens here and in other countries thus carrying out the President's wish to spread over the world the benefits of our free type of civilization.[34]

---

[33] Letter to Secretary of the Treasury John W. Snyder, 1950.

[34] Ibid.

5

FDR

McKenna considered the action of eliminating the gold standard by President Roosevelt to be simply unforgivable. Based on two pre-election speeches by FDR, McKenna believed Roosevelt knew the public wanted sound money, but intentionally mislead voters to win the election.

> You have seen many strange things during your lifetime. Let us blink our eyes and take a second look at how we were tricked into going off the gold standard. Our eyes behold a presidential candidate winning the election on a platform pledged to economy in Federal government and maintenance of the gold standard. Let me read to you from the campaign speeches of F.D. Roosevelt in 1932. On July 30, 1932 at Albany he said, 'Let us have the courage to stop borrowing to meet continuing deficits. Stop the deficits. Let us have the courage to reverse the policy of the Republican leaders and insist on a sound currency. . . . This concerns you my friends, who managed to lay aside a few dollars for a rainy day.' And on November 4, 1932, only four days before election day he said, 'The businessmen of the country, battling hard to maintain their financial solvency and integrity were told in blunt language in Des Moines, Iowa by the President (then Hoover) how close an escape this country had some months ago from going off the gold standard. This, as has been clearly shown since, was a libel on the credit of the United States. No adequate response was made to the magnificent philippic of Carter Glass the other night which showed how false was that assertion. And I might add, Senator Glass made a devastating challenge that no responsible government would have sold to the country securities payable in gold if he knew that the promise, yes the covenant, embodied in those securities was as dubious as the President of the United States (Hoover) claims it was.' Later in that same speech Roosevelt said, 'The Democratic platform specifically declares 'We advocate a sound currency to be prescribed at all hazards. That is plain English. In discussing this platform on July 30, 1932, I

> said, Sound Money is an international necessity; not a domestic consideration for one nation alone. In other words I want to see sound money in all the world.' Certainly we Americans who elected a President on that platform did not give any mandate to him to foist the curse of irredeemable paper upon us within less than a year from the time he made those statements.[35]

After rallying votes by promising sound money to America, as noted by McKenna, Roosevelt quickly criminalized the private ownership of gold and devalued the dollar almost 70 percent. This directly contradicted his campaign promises and disenfranchised Americans of an estimable portion of their liquid wealth.

Ending the gold standard, was not the only disagreement McKenna had with FDR. McKenna also blamed FDR for the "creeping socialism" that has increasingly afflicted the United States. McKenna felt there was a causal relationship between the abolition of the convertible gold standard and the rise of socialism in America.

McKenna's ideological conflict with FDR was typical of the businessmen of his era. According to Gary M. Walton and Hugh Rockoff:

> most of the criticism was directed toward the antibusiness political climate created by the Roosevelt administration, which, it was asserted, made vigorous business expansion impossible.... Why would business undertake long-term investments, the critics of the administration

---

[35]McKenna M., Philip, "Our Need for the Gold Standard In a War Economy," an address delivered September 21, 1950 before the National Association of Cost Accounts, Detroit Chapter, at the Hotel Sheraton, Detroit, Michigan, p. 5. Friedman and Schwartz confirm FDR's election campaign statements ". . . which were interpreted—certainly by Senator Glass, among other—as committing himself [Roosevelt] to the retention of the gold standard at the then existing gold parity" (Milton Friedman and Anna J. Schwartz, *A Monetary History of the United States, 1867–1960*, Princeton University Press, Princeton, 1963, pp. 331–332). Friedman and Schwartz (footnote number 45 on page 332) also noted the disapproval of Senator Glass when FDR reversed his position on gold-backed money.

> wondered, when the profits might all be taken away by future legislation.[36]

In 1997, the United States Mint issued a 5 dollar gold coin in honor of FDR. On the face of the coin is FDR's head and on the back of the coin is FDR's 1933 Inaugural Seal. We would not want to venture what Philip M. McKenna's remarks would be on this tribute.

---

[36] Walton, Gary M. and Rockoff, Hugh, *History of the American Economy*, The Dryden Press, Fort Worth, 1994, p. 533.

6

Government Control of Hard Money

In 1952, McKenna wrote a letter to the Editor of *The American Banker* in which he expresses his distrust of the government being in charge of all hard money. *The American Banker* evidently printed an editorial advocating the use of silver dollars to prevent inflation, but called for the silver to be used only when paying for imports, and thus not circulated in America. It was with this aspect of the editorial that McKenna took issue. He writes in his letter,

> Your concluding paragraph, 'One thing which has been needed in China for 20 years, and is needed in Korea and other nations, is a plentitude of hard money to move in trade and commerce. Paper currency has been a horrible snare and delusion to the peoples of the Pacific East. Silver money might do more to make capitalists of them all than all the propaganda we could muster,' is very true. Yes, indeed Korea and other nations need hard money. One of those nations needing hard money is the USA! But the Treasury and the Federal Reserve Bankers don't think the place for hard money is 'jingling in the pockets' of the people. The word 'jingling' implies that people are careless with their money, while the government knows better how to use it! At any rate, the bankers, by 1932, had assisted in inveigling most of the gold coins out of the possession of people. They did it by casting aspersions, *obloquy*, and regarding as queer, citizens who in 1927 and 1928 asked for a few gold coins at the tellers' windows, instead of putting it into the hands of 'capable and competent men' who invested it for them in various projects on which they got a commission. The bankers forgot that those who do not protect, encourage and uphold the freedom of others will lose their own freedom. It was easy for the government to take the gold away from the bankers, who because of the misbehavior of some of them and the political propaganda directed

> toward finding a 'goat' other than misgovernment, put the bankers 'in the doghouse' by 1933.

Specie currency is often prescribed as a stabilizing medicine for countries that are undergoing severe currency fluctuations, but seldom for countries in a period of relative stability. Much like citrus fruit and scurvy, a gold standard can provide countries with the monetary stability necessary to avoid becoming economically unstable. After economies under fiat currencies collapse, the infusion of a gold standard is painful, and often too late to avoid serious suffering. McKenna sought to readopt a gold standard early, and everywhere, to avoid economic crisis rather than just as a remedy after disaster strikes.

7

"The Monsters of Man's Creation"[37]

McKenna questioned government's resolve to stabilize a currency by managing the size of the money supply.

> Can you name for me an instance in all of the times irredeemable paper currency has been tried in historical or modern times, that it went any other way than downward in purchasing power until it became worthless, or was made convertible again, generally in a much lower weight of precious metal?[38]

McKenna understood the political realities of appeasing special interest groups with "pork-barrel" expenditures,

> Log-rolling politicians to gain favor with first one section of the electorate and then another vote for subsidies, grants and other expenditures, which can only be made up by deficit spending, that is by dipping into the public purse beyond the amount which can be collected in taxes authorized by the representatives of the people.[39]

According to McKenna, the reason FDR took us off the gold standard was to raise an extra $2 billion in revenues (raising the price of gold to $35 per ounce, allowed the Federal Reserve to print more money) "to buy favor politically . . ."[40]

---

[37] Letter to Dr. Edwin G. Nourse, April 13, 1950.

[38] Letter to George Putnam, August 3, 1950.

[39] Ibid.

[40] Letter to Dr. Edwin Nourse, April 13, 1950.

Philip McKenna also cites the historical case of France where between 1914 and 1950 the franc lost 98% of its value. "It was done by the politicians in France to maintain themselves and their supporters in public office in the style to which they [had] become accustomed and was possible only because they robbed the thrifty, diligent and trusting people by inflation."[41]

McKenna noted that a gold standard forces governments to be fiscally responsible, which results in lower taxes, which results in more inventions and risk taking.

> Federal financial responsibility, to McKenna, means lower taxes, and that would mean more money for McKenna. He wants it badly. And why he wants it is best shown in his own words: 'Science is best served in the field of invention by sound money and economic freedom to risk it.'[42]

---

[41] Letter to George Putnam, August 3, 1950.

[42] "For Hot Jets: A Man and a Gun," *Business Week*, September 20, 1952.

8

Congressional Proposals to Return to the Gold Standard

During the years of the Gold Standard League's existence there were several bills proposed in both the House and Senate which aimed to restore some aspect of the gold standard.[43] The Gold Standard League actively promoted these bills, but urged its members to write to their Senators and Congressmen in support of the preferred HR 3262 gold standard bill.

One congressman, interested in the issue of sound money, was Senator Harry P. Cain. On March 6, 1950, McKenna wrote a letter to Senator Cain responding to Cain's address before the National Association of Home Builders on February 22, 1950. McKenna also refers to Cain's May 6, 1949 pro gold responses at the hearing on S 13 of The Banking & Currency Committee. The letter goes on to give the Senator some advice, "Get the government out of business which they don't understand and we'll provide employment for my boys in Latrobe, Pennsylvania, and we'll improve living standards here and abroad." McKenna did not like Cain's suggestion that gold be traded freely in the open market on a temporary basis, rather he preferred that gold be permanently traded in the open market.

---

[43] When the Gold Standard League was first formed, McKenna was very optimistic about the United States returning to a gold standard. The Swiss had voted in May 1949 to return the gold standard and the Swiss National Bank (Switzerland's central bank) was required to convert its banknotes to gold on demand after January 1, 1950.

> You [Cain] hadn't grasped the idea that as the Constitution said 'Congress shall have the power to coin money and regulate the value thereof,' by which they meant the weight of precious metal in a dollar. Just get that fixed, and redeemable and you've restored freedom. Do not be misled by those who tell you that with 2% of the supply on the market and 98% withheld by our Treasury you can have a free market. **Gold is a monetary metal.**

He wanted Cain to support HR 3262 which would have restored the gold standard and allowed gold to be redeemed at $35 per ounce. He explained to Cain how gold encourages savings, "nobody hoards gold when the government is honest and redeems its money in gold at our standard of value." If the dollar were redeemable, McKenna concludes, it would be better to ". . .buy government bonds, they'll pay you 2% in **real value**. . . ."

McKenna was upset that the U.S. Treasury was paying out gold bullion to foreign central banks at $35 per ounce but would not sell gold to its own citizens. If there was a free market, as Cain proposes, foreigners would be allowed to sell gold to U.S. residents at a premium above the $35. However, McKenna recognized that a two-tiered price system would not work: "Will they [Treasury] continue to make good to foreign central banks at $35?" "It was our work that gave value to the dollar that caused the gold to come into our Treasury to get dollars for purchasing the product of our toil and risk-taking."

This theme occurs again in McKenna's August, 1950 letter to George Putnam, which addresses Mr. Putnam's proposal to ". . . continue the $35-an-ounce price of gold for all that is produced domestically, but to maintain no bid on gold that is mined outside the U.S.A. . . ." This, argued McKenna, would create a two-price system for gold, "one for foreign gold and $35 an ounce for domestically mined gold." This was problematic because it would

> provide an incentive to smuggling and fraud, building up a class of outlaws similar but more powerful than the gangsters created by

Prohibition.[44] Doubtless they would soon be conniving with powerful politicians corrupting our country again. The urge to hold gold is impelled by two very powerful emotions, fear and avarice. Fear of inflation is well grounded in view of all history of irredeemable paper money. It is shared by the thoughtful, those having foresight and of a provident nature. Thus the illegal operations would have the support of otherwise law abiding citizens. Denied the protection for their savings afforded only by an honest currency, redeemable in something of intrinsic value, they would protect themselves by illegal means. Joined with them would be the class who have an intense love of gain, however obtained. It is sad that to protect themselves and their families and dependents from predatory government and to obtain that protection which should be afforded every citizen by our government, under the Constitution, men would have to pay a premium for the standard of money which Congress is empowered to establish by straight forward coining of gold at a regulated weight of precious metal per dollar.

[44] He cites the example of gold being smuggled out of mines in Canada (official price of $38.50 per ounce) because of higher "underworld prices" offered by "high-graders." He also discusses a historical example—Lord Cunliffe, chairman of the Bullion Commission in 1819, "remarked that the oath of an Englishman could be accurately evaluated at 14 percent!" As noted by McKenna, prior to England's adoption of one price for gold, they were paying slightly more than the face value of the British gold coins. As a consequence, coins were melted down and sold back to the Treasury. Englanders selling gold to the Bank took an oath "that it had been produced or imported and had not been obtained by melting down coin!" (August 3, 1950, letter to George Putnam)

9

Gold as a Standard of Value

The importance of a standard of value is a theme that echoes throughout many of McKenna's writings. Without a stable monetary measurement tool, all monetary transactions become risky. This risk translates into inefficient transactions involving high interest rates and/or even barter.

> . . . the gold standard is like providing sound rails for a railroad—it won't prevent wrecks, but it's necessary for a good railroad. It is available for the use of honest men in deferred transactions. . . . It enables men to carry on business, especially in deferred transactions, wherein someone saves up money for the provision of tools such as machine tools, relying upon being paid back in a definite value. 'The promises men live by' cannot be carried on very well without the gold standard.[45]

According to McKenna, the lack of a consistent standard of value, added to the graduated income tax, results in businessmen who are reluctant to make investments for fear of not obtaining the projected returns.

On March 20, 1950, McKenna wrote a letter to the members of the Gold Standard League who were bankers, in response to a speech by Senator Cain calling for a show of support from bankers for a return to the gold standard. In the letter he chastises the American Banker's Association for not becoming more active in the move to restore the gold standard:

---

[45] Letter to Dr. Edwin Nourse, April 13, 1950.

> Probably the primary responsibility for urging honest money rests upon the American Banker's Association. This body has consistently, so far as I know, remained silent on the great issue of currency. I have never seen the Association become indignant or express any articulate opposition to what is happening to our American dollar. In my view their silence implies a bypassing of their moral responsibility to the millions of American who are their depositors.

When Americans finally realize the loss of savings due to inflation, McKenna claims, "They may flock to a demagogue like Hitler who will promise to redress their grievance by force and a new form of society, generally a dictatorship, whether of the proletariat or of other groups will ensue." Thus the consequences of inflation cannot be eliminated via inflation hedging assets. "Those who imagined themselves clever, and who bought common shares, equities and real estate, thinking they might actually benefit by inflation will be cruelly undeceived by rent fixing, seizure of property and confiscation until they flee the country."

In an October, 1950 letter to Walter Lichtenstein, a professor at Harvard University and university librarian, McKenna again expressed his fear that irredeemable money would lead to "great losses to the thrifty, trustful and conservative middle class." These, individuals, thus weakened, would become prey to dictators. McKenna went on to explain that he believed this did not have to happen in America.

> I believe Americans are capable of raising up a standard which will build up a system based upon the Judeo-Christian ethic that the individual human being is the building block which is worthy of protection as a creature of God, while man-made entities such as governments based on power alone, monopolies in banking, in labor union monopolies and other organized aggressions are merely products of weak and fallible men and thus may and should be dissolved or decentralized . . . I regard it as the duty of Americans who have the knowledge to do it, to tell others of the consequences of irredeemable paper money such as we have now. I am not content merely to be a philosopher recording the decline of human liberty in America. On the contrary I think it is

inevitable that the American people will regain it. The 'experiment' of irredeemable currency will go into the limbo of other 'noble experiments' like Prohibition. How much damage is done to our institutions and social structure before the reform is made depends upon how soon the American people become alerted to the danger of deterioration.

10

Conclusions

Although intently focused on economic policy and political economy, one can see that McKenna's public philosophy and political principles were much broader. He understood that the success of America's economy was based on its political order: "The strength of American industry, nurtured on Constitutional freedom and still deriving its relative strength from 175 years of freedom . . ."[46]

McKenna sought the traditional values of a healthy society—life, property, liberty and the pursuit of happiness—and believed that they could only be assured under capitalism and adherence to a strict gold coin standard. Human liberty is sacred in McKenna's eyes. It must be vigilantly protected from government infringements—the gold standard is a free society's keystone. "Sound currency redeemable in gold is just another necessary tool of free men. In fact, for lack of it the system by which we develop such values as we enjoy will be destroyed."[47]

The gold standard proffers two advantages over current fiat regimes: price stability[48] and fiscally honest government. Foremost,

---

[46] Letter to "Dear Boys," August 30, 1947.

[47] Philip M. McKenna, "How to Return to the Gold Standard Now," lecture presented at the International Gold Coin Conference in New York City, Sept., 1949.

[48] The obvious caveat here is that prices are stable as long as the growth of the central bank's holdings of gold approximates long-term real income growth (given that we hold the price of gold constant relative to the domestic currency) or we are willing to revalue (devalue) gold to allow for the printing of the fiat

a gold standard offers price stability by hindering monetary manipulation by governments in the pursuit of short-term popularity. We have numerous examples, both past and present, of the results of such monetary mischief. Recent financial crises in developing countries (e.g., Thailand, Indonesia, Malaysia, Brazil and Russia) have led to 40 percent plus currency devaluations which, in turn, have led to a loss of confidence in the domestic currency,

---

currency in cases of deflationary (inflationary) pressures.

Friedman and Schwartz note two periods of time where gold discoveries led to significant increases in prices: In the early 1850s, there was a large increase in prices when gold was discovered in California, and from 1897 to 1914, prices increased at an average rate of 2 percent per year—the dollar lost a total of 40 percent of its purchasing power—due to gold discoveries in "South Africa, Alaska, and Colorado and from the development of improved methods of mining and refining" (Milton Friedman and Anna J. Schwartz, *A Monetary History of the United States*, 1867–1960, Princeton University Press, Princeton, 1963, p. 137).

The second, even more dramatic price change, occurred from 1929 to 1933, while the United States was on a gold standard, wholesale prices dropped 25 percent and real net national product dropped 33 percent. However, it is true that the Federal Reserve was sterilizing gold inflows, during this time period, which would have prevented some of the price decrease. Once we exited the gold standard in 1933, the monetary base increased 12.2 percent per year from 1933 to April 1936. As a consequence, from 1933 to May of 1937, real income increased at a 9 percent rate per year and inflation edged up to an annual rate of 2.8 percent. Unfortunately, from 1936 to 1937, the Federal Reserve over responded to the inflation by doubling the reserve requirement ratio between August 1936 and May of 1937 while simultaneously sterilizing gold inflows during the first nine months of 1937 (Friedman and Schwartz, p. 510 and Darby, Michael R. and Melvin, Michael T., *Intermediate Macroeconomics,* Scott, Foresman and Company, Illinois, 1987, pp. 374–384). The growth rate of the monetary base in 1937 plummeted to an annual rate of 3 percent (Friedman and Schwartz, p. 804, Table B-3). Furthermore, FDR raised taxes in a misguided attempt to balance the budget. Real GNP growth contracted once again and unemployment rates shot up to 17 percent.

For a review of the economic history of the Great Depression and the New Deal see Darby, Michael R. and Melvin, Michael T., pp. 374–384; Walton, Gary M. and Rockoff, Hugh, *History of the American Economy*, The Dryden Press, Fort Worth, 1994, pp. 515–557; and Friedman and Schwartz, Chapters 7–8.

capital outflows, and economic chaos. Sound money is the foundation for healthy government and industry as much now as it was during McKenna's time.

Secondly, the gold standard keeps governments honest by eliminating the tendency to tax us through deficit financing. In as much as direct taxation becomes politically difficult and unpopular, indirect taxation through the inflation of nonconvertible currency becomes attractive. Such inflation constitutes a hidden regressive tax.

Admittedly, most contemporary monetary theorists (e.g., Friedman, Schwartz, Darby, Melvin, and McCallum) believe that the gold standard was too restrictive during the 1930s and partially to blame for the collapse of commodity and wholesale prices and consequently some of the drop in real output that occurred. These economists may not share McKenna's views on the necessity of having gold to anchor our monetary system, but they would agree, whole heartedly with Philip McKenna's observations on the mismanagement of monetary policy conducted by the Federal Reserve System during the Great Depression and ineptness of FDR's and Hoover's fiscal policies. According to Darby and Melvin, "The Great Depression provides a startling example of the destabilizing potential of macroeconomic policy [e.g., the Smoot-Hawley Tariff, an overly restrictive monetary policy, failure of the Fed to act as a lender-of-last-resort as indicated by the permitted failure of the Bank of the United States and the collapse of one-third of the commercial banks in the United States from 1929 to 1933, Hoover raising taxes in 1932, FDR raising taxes in 1936, and so on]."[49]

Furthermore, it must be noted that most contemporary economists and Americans in general would not challenge McKenna's views on the public's right to own gold. But this observation is too myopic—McKenna's philosophical testimonials

---

[49] Darby, Michael R. and Melvin, Michael T., *Intermediate Macroeconomics*, Scott, Foresman and Company, Illinois, 1987, p. 383.

and harbinger warnings about the ever-growing losses to personal freedom via government infringements on personal property rights ("creeping socialism") have become an increasing concern to millions of Americans.

Many members of the Gold Standard League, including McKenna, as well as other concerned citizens, testified before the sub-committee of the Senate Committee on Banking and Currency from March 29 through April 1, 1954. When the Senate adjourned, McKenna had reached his limit and thoughtfully noted that he and perhaps the Gold Standard League had done all that they were capable of doing and that others would have to finish the battle.

> After the Senate went home, without having done anything about it I considered what more could be done. I have come to the conclusion that a majority of American citizens want the gold coin standard as a protection to themselves, their families and their businesses and institutions. . . . The issue is much bigger than can be expressed effectively by the association of persons in our tiny League. There are monetary economists able and willing to draft good and accurate bills and answer legal and technical questions regarding monetary law and policy.

McKenna announced his resignation as National Chairman of the Gold Standard League and from membership in the League on January 15, 1955. In addition to limiting his activities for health reasons, he also had come to believe that the work of the League had accomplished one important objective: "to inform the people of the necessity for the gold standard with a redeemable currency." He concluded his resignation letter by urging his fellow Gold Standard League members to continue working for monetary reform: "Each of us who wants the fundamental honesty of the gold coin standard of money and sees the danger of continuing any longer without it can, as an individual, in his own way, voice his opinion." "The Gold Standard League was merged into the

Economists' National Committee on Monetary Policy" which continued McKenna's work.[50]

[50] Philip M. McKenna Memorial Tablet Dedication Service, August 16, 1970.

Appendix

Philip Mowry McKenna

An internationally known engineer, metallurgist, scientist . . ., Philip Mowry McKenna was perhaps best known for his invention of the first commercially successful steel-cutting carbide. This was based on his research in the 1930's which resulted in the discovery of the inter-metallic compound tungsten-titanium carbide ($WTiC_2$) upon which patents were granted in 1938. During his lifetime he [Philip] was issued 35 patents, the first in 1913 at the age of sixteen, and the last on April 23, 1968 two years before his death.

Born in Pittsburgh, Pennsylvania, on June 16, 1897, Philip McKenna was the son of Alexander George McKenna, one of the most respected metallurgists of his day and a pioneer in the development of high-speed tool steel. While attending high school in Washington, D.C., he worked at the United States Bureau of Standards, and at age 19 he became vice president and general manager of chemical Products of Washington, D.C. He was graduated from George Washington University in 1921 with a degree in chemistry.

In the 1920's, he served as a consultant for various companies, attended California Institute of Technology, and began the research that culminated in his major discoveries. In 1928, he became research director and vice president of Vanadium Alloys Steel Company, Latrobe, Pa., a company which his father had helped to found. He remained with Vanadium until 1938, at which time he founded his own business, McKenna Metals Co., and began the production of 'Kennametal,' the trade-name he had adopted for his revolutionary new tool materials.

. . .

The business, originally operated as a proprietorship and then partnership, was incorporated as Kennametal Inc. in 1943. Its sales grew from thirty thousand in 1938 to almost ten million dollars in 1945 . . .

. . .

For his accomplishments, Philip McKenna was given many honors. In 1953, the American society of Mechanical Engineers conferred two honors on him—its Holley Medal and Towne Lectureship. The Holley Medal (previously awarded to such men as Henry Ford, Herbert Hoover, Elmer Sperry, Ernest Lawrence and Vannevar Bush) was given him 'for a great and unique act of genius of an engineering nature that has accomplished a timely benefit . . . for the discovery of principles and the development of new processes in the application of distinctive types of tool materials resulting in great improvements in metal cutting.' He was chosen to deliver the 1953 Towne Lecture in recognition of his leadership in monetary economics.

In 1955, the American Society of Tool Engineers presented Philip McKenna with its Engineering Citation of the year. The award was in recognition of Mr. McKenna's 'original and important contributions to the development of carbide materials and tools, and their application in the machining and forming of manufacturing materials.' The citation also recognized him as an 'able worker for the advancement of science and the public welfare.'

Phillip McKenna was a man of action and had unbounded enthusiasm for the things in which he believed. He had a very strong belief in the virtues of the free enterprise system and in the ability of men to create and produce best in a free, competitive society. He recognized that cooperation among men was the key to great accomplishments. . . . He gave a large measure of both time and money in an earnest attempt to protect our economic freedom and constitutional liberties.

. . .

Those who knew him—worked with him—and learned from him—will always remember Philip M. McKenna as an inspiring leader and a great and good friend.[51]

Philip McKenna was a true intellectual who read widely of many subjects. His library contained James Madison's *Journal of the Federal Convention*, Voltaire's *Candide*, and works by Tennyson, Sir Walter Scott, Charles Dickens, Jules Verne, T.E. Lawrence, John Milton, Rudyard Kipling, and many others. He could both read and write French fluently. The books and authors that most influenced his public policy writings include, F.A. Hayek's *The Road to Serfdom*, John Maynard Keynes' *General Theory*, Ludwig

---

[51] Ibid.

von Mises' *Human Action* and *The Theory of Money and Credit*, and Andrew Dickson White's *Fiat Money Inflation in France*.

He carried on relations and networked with many of the conservative and influential leaders of his day, including Congressman Howard Buffett (Warren's father); Congressman Daniel E. Reed of New York, the ranking republican member of the House Committee on Banking and Currency; Senator Francis Case[52] of South Dakota; Senator Edward Martin of Pennsylvania; Senator Harry P. Cain ("Hurry Cain") of Washington; Senator Harry Byrd[53] of Virginia; Dr. Edwin G. Nourse, Chair of the Council of Economic Advisors from 1946 to 1949; Henry S. Hazlitt, "literary editor at *The Nation*, top editorialist at the *New York Times*, and a weekly columnist at *Newsweek*"[54]; Felix Morely, one of the founders of *Human Events*; Leonard Reed, the founder of Foundation for Economic Education; Frank Chodorov,[55] one of the founders of the Intercollegiate Studies Institute; Vic Milione, former president of the Intercollegiate Studies Institute; Dr. Walter Spahr,[56] chair of the economics department, from 1928 to 1956, at New York University and one of the founders and executive secretary of the Economists' National Committee on Monetary Policy; Dr. Walter Lichtenstein, professor at Harvard University and university librarian; Dr. Vannevar Bush, faculty member, vice-president and dean at MIT; Dr. Glenn Olin Saxon,[57] professor of economics at Yale University from 1931 to 1961; Rev. Armand Jean Baldwin,[58] chair of the Political Science and Economics

---

[52] See photo number 29.

[53] See photo number 34.

[54] See Rockwell, Jr., Llewellyn, "Henry Hazlitt: Journalist of the Century," *The Freeman: Ideas on Liberty*, The Foundation for Economic Freedom, May 1995, p. 276–281. See photo number 32.

[55] See photo number 30.

[56] See photo number 33.

[57] See photo number 32.

[58] See photo number 31.

departments at Saint Vincent College; George Putnam of the George Putnam Fund of Boston; Tom Howes, assistant Secretary of the Treasury under Secretary William Woodin (authored the Banking Act of 1933, which took the U.S. off the Gold Standard); and Barry Goldwater. He also corresponded with Ludwig von Mises, Austrian Economist and visiting professor at New York University from 1948 to 1969.[59] It was Philip M. McKenna who provided the funding that made possible the "New Edition" of *The Theory of Money and Credit* which was published by Yale University Press in 1953.[60]

Mr. McKenna was on the board of Americans for Constitutional Action, a national organization whose objective was to repeal the federal income tax. He was a nationally known advocate of conservative economics.

Philip M. McKenna died August 17, 1969. He was a serious man of public affairs with strong personal commitments to a principled life.

---

[59] *The Fortune Encyclopedia of Economics*, ed. Henderson, David R., Warner Books, New York, 1993, pp. 818–819.

[60] Photos 1 and 2 reveal two letters confirming McKenna's financial contribution to Mises' book.

Officers and State Chairmen of the Gold Standard League in 1941

National Chairman: Philip M. McKenna
Treasurer: George T. Kearns
Executive Secretary: Zack R. Cecil
State Chairmen:

Alabama	David R. Dunlap *Chairman of the Corporation,* *Alabama Dry Dock and Shipbuilding Co.*
Connecticut	James W. Knox
Florida	R.V. Walker *Savings and Loan Executive*
Georgia	Julian N. Barrett *Investment Broker*
Indiana	J.L. Brenn *President, Huntington Laboratories, Inc.*
Massachusetts	Leland Powers *Attorney*
Michigan	Fred Marin *President, Bank of Lansing*
Nebraska	Dean Krotter *Farmer and Industrialist*
New York	Philip LeBoutellier *President and General Manager, Best and Co.*
Ohio	J. Keller Kirn *Banker*
Texas	J.H. Frost *Chairman of the Board* *Frost National Bank*
Wisconsin	E.B. Tilton *Industrialist and Economist*

Assisting:

George F. Bauer
Addision W. Arthurs
Donald C. McKenna
Lawrence L. McKenna

80TH CONGRESS
2D Session

H. R. 5031

IN THE HOUSE OF REPRESENTATIVES

January 20, 1948
Mr. Buffett introduced the following bill; which was referred to the Committee on Banking and Currency

A BILL

To restore the right of American citizens to freely own gold and gold coins; to return control over the public purse to the people; to restrain further deterioration of our currency; to enable holders of paper money to redeem it in gold coin on demand; to establish and maintain a domestic gold coin standard; and for other purposes.

Be it enacted by the Senate and House of Representatives of the United States of America in Congress assembled, This Act may be cited as the "Gold Standard Act of 1948."

SEC. 2. The standard monetary unit of the United States of America shall be the gold dollar of fifteen and five twenty-one one-hundredths grains nine-tenths fine. Gold coins of not less than

$10 denomination and such larger denominations as the Secretary of the Treasury finds desirable shall be minted and issued upon demand.

SEC. 3. Nothing in this Act shall be construed to change the size, weight, or fineness of the present lawful silver coins.

SEC. 4. Standard gold coin and gold certificates shall be full legal tender.

SEC. 5. All other money of the United States shall be maintained on a parity with the standard gold dollar by freedom of exchanges at par with standard gold.

SEC. 6. Standard gold bullion and coin as well as gold certificates shall be lawful money for reserves against deposits in Federal Reserve banks and in 5 per centum redemption fund against Federal Reserve notes.

SEC. 7. Standard gold bullion and coin as well as gold certificates shall count as part of the minimum reserve of 25 per centum to be held by Federal Reserve banks against their Federal Reserve notes in actual circulation.

SEC. 8. All legally issued Treasury currency, except (a) fractional silver and minor coins as provided in section 9, and (b) bank notes and Treasury notes in the process of retirement, shall have the quality of full legal tender. Specifically, the following shall have the quality of full legal tender: Gold coin and gold certificates, silver dollars and silver certificates, and United States notes.

SEC. 9. Fractional silver coins shall be legal tender only up to $10. Five-cent pieces and one-cent pieces shall be legal tender only up to 25 cents.

SEC. 10. Federal Reserve notes shall be receivable for all debts, public and private, but they may not be counted as reserves against other notes or deposits of issuing banks.

SEC. 11. All provisions of law authorizing the President to alter the size, weight, or fineness of gold and silver coins are hereby repealed. The mint charges for assaying and coining gold and silver, limits of tolerance, and the alloys in gold and silver coins shall be those in effect in 1932.

SEC. 12. That part of section 43 of the Act of May 12, 1933, as amended by Public Resolution Numbered 10, approved June 5, 1933, providing that all coins and currencies of the United States shall be full legal tender, is hereby repealed.

SEC. 13. The Act of June 12, 1945 (59 Stat. 237), is hereby amended to provide that all Treasury currency, except that in process of retirement, shall be counted along with gold and gold certificates, as part of the lawful money for reserves against deposits in Federal Reserve banks. Specifically, all silver and minor coins, silver certificates, and United States notes shall be added to gold and gold certificates as part of the money that is lawful for reserves in Federal Reserve banks against their deposits.

SEC. 14. The Gold Reserve Act of 1934 (48 Stat. 337) is hereby repealed.

SEC. 15. This Act shall take effect January 20, 1949.

81ST CONGRESS
1ST SESSION

H.R. 3262

IN THE HOUSE OF REPRESENTATIVES

March 7, 1949

Mr. Reed of New York introduced the following bill; which was referred to the Committee on Banking and Currency

A BILL

To restore the right of American citizens to freely own gold and gold coins; to return control over the public purse to the people; to restrain further deterioration of our currency; to enable holders of paper money to redeem it in gold coin on demand; to establish and maintain a domestic gold coin standard; and for other purposes.

Be it enacted by the Senate and House of Representatives of the United States of America in Congress assembled, That this Act may be cited as the "Gold Standard Act of 1949."

SEC. 2. The standard monetary unit of the United States of America shall be the gold dollar of fifteen and twenty-firsts grains nine-tenths fine. Gold coins not less than $10 denominations as the Secretary of the Treasury finds desirable shall be minted and issued upon demand.

SEC. 3. Nothing in this Act shall be construed to change the size, weight, or fineness of the present lawful silver coins.

SEC. 4. Standard gold coin and gold certificates shall be full legal tender.

SEC. 5. All other money of the United States shall be maintained on a parity with the standard gold dollar by freedom of exchanges at par with standard gold.

SEC. 6. Standard gold bullion and coin as well as gold certificates shall be lawful money for reserves against deposits in Federal Reserve banks and in the 5 per centum redemption fund against Federal Reserve notes.

SEC. 7. Standard gold bullion and coin as well as gold certificates shall not count as part of the minimum reserve of 25 per centum to be held by Federal Reserve banks against their Federal Reserve notes in actual circulation.

SEC. 8. All legally issued Treasury currency, except (a) fractional silver and minor coins as provided in section 9, and (b) bank notes and Treasury notes in the process of retirement, shall have the quality of full legal tender. Specifically, the following shall have the quality of full legal tender: Gold coin and gold certificates, silver dollars and silver certificates, and United States notes.

SEC. 9. Fractional silver coins shall be legal tender only up to $10. Five-cent pieces shall be legal tender only up to 25 cents.

SEC. 10. Federal Reserve notes shall be receivable for all debts, public and private, but they may not be counted as reserves against other notes or deposits of issuing banks.

SEC. 11. All provisions of law authorizing the President to alter the size, weight, or fineness of gold and silver coins are hereby repealed. The mint charges for assaying and coining gold and silver, limits of tolerance, and the alloys in gold and silver coins shall be those in effect in 1932.

SEC. 12. That part of section 43 of the Act of May 12, 1933, as amended by Public Resolution Numbered 10, approved

June 5, 1933, providing that all coins and currencies of the United States shall be full legal tender, is hereby repealed.

SEC. 13. The Act of June 12, 1945 (59 Stat. 237), is hereby amended to provide that all Treasury currency except that in process of retirement, shall be counted along with gold and gold certificates, as part of the lawful money for reserves against deposits in Federal Reserve banks. Specifically all silver and minor coins, silver certificates, and United States notes shall be added to gold and gold certificates, as part of the money that is lawful for reserves in Federal Reserve banks against their deposits.

SEC. 14. The Gold Reserve Act of 1934 (48 Stat. 337) is hereby repealed.

SEC. 15. This Act shall take effect June 30, 1950.

McKenna Photos

and

Pro Gold Standard Advertisements

LUDWIG VON MISES
777 WEST END AVENUE
NEW YORK 25, N.Y.

December 22, 1951

Mr. Zack R. Cecil
The Gold Standard League
One Lloyd Avenue
Latrobe, Pa

Dear Mr. Cecil:

Thanks for your letter of December 14. I appreciate very highly your and the Gold Standard League's help in publishing a new edition of my book on Money. I hope everything will turn our in full accord with the scheme developed at our meeting at the Biltmore.

It will be a great pleasure for me to see you at my planned lecture-series in San Francisco.

Best wishes for a Merry Christmas and a Happy New Year to you and Mrs. Cecil, also from Mrs. Mises.

Sincerely yours

L. Mises

photo 1

December 27, 1951

Dr. Ludwig von Mises
777 West End Avenue
New York 25, New York

Dear Dr. von Mises:

The publication of "The Theory Of Money And Credit" has been officially settled as far as we are concerned and the principal who will make publication possible and through whom all transactions pertaining to the publication, other than Yale University Press, will be The American Economic Foundation and Mr. Richard Rimanoczy will handle the matter. Credit for publication belongs entirely to Mr. Philip M. McKenna who has made the funds available. It is true, I urged the project but it is his generosity that makes the project possible.

The matter is out of my hands, but Mr. Davidson seemed to thank that there would be some reluctance in putting forth special promotion on the book. You will recall that a tentative figure of $1,500 was proffered them for this project. This amount has been made available to the Foundation and we want to be sure that either Yale University Press or the Foundation carries out that part of the project. Davidson seemed to think that the subject was so controversial, which is silly, that Yale University Press would receive a bad reaction if they made a special effort to sell the book.

I do hope that the new introduction is being prepared and the project being pushed for completion. You will no doubt hear from Mr. Rimanoczy.

Mrs. Cecil and I extend the Season's Greetings to you and Mrs. von Mises. We are hopeful that the San Francisco project can be accomplished.

Sincerely yours,

Zack R. Cecil

ZRC/pt

photo 2

photo 3

photo 4

Gold Standard League meeting.

photo 5

McKenna demonstrating how the United States monetary system operates under a fiat system.

photo 6

photo 7

Displays created by the Gold Standard League

This is a *Fast Turning* Job

From Which No One Derives a Profit

It may be fun for a puppy to pursue its appendage—but when the puppy is wages and the tail is prices, the situation is serious.

Once in a while the puppy catches the tail—but the strain is too great. So, prices break away—and the mad scramble is on again.

What causes the price-wages spiral?

The selfish interest of management, or labor? No, we think not. After all—both groups are composed of good citizens. And, as good citizens, each is entitled to receive fair pay for work done, plus a reasonable reserve to insure future security.

Is it, then, that the intrinsic cost of goods is becoming greater and greater? No. Modern tools of production enable one man and one machine to produce as much as 5 times more than they did 10 years ago.*

What, then? We might as well face the fact—the value of money is becoming less and less. A deteriorating currency is a basic cause of price rises—and wage increases are required to offset them.

The convertible gold standard is not perfect but it is the most practical and reliable measure of value ever devised. It provides the essential inflexible yardstick by which values may be compared, and commitments made with actual, as well as implied integrity.

A bill has been introduced in the Congress to restore stability to the dollar, making all currency freely convertible to gold. We suggest you write your Congressman for a copy of H. R. Bill 5031, study it, and take action.

* Kennametal tooling makes it practicable to machine steel and cast iron at cutting speeds up to 10 times faster than those possible with steel tools; take interrupted cuts on steel and cast iron at the same speeds used for continuous cutting; cut steel in the hardened state, thereby often eliminating annealing and rehardening operations, and . . . turn out from two to five times as much as high speed steel tools on the same machine and in the same time.

This Bill is Needed to Guarantee a Reliable Index of Individual and Corporate Profit

H. R. 5031

To restore the right of American citizens to freely own gold and gold coins; to return control over the public purse to the people; to restrain further deterioration of our currency; to enable holders of paper money to redeem it in gold coin on demand; to establish and maintain a domestic gold coin standard; and for other purposes.

KENNAMETAL *Inc.*
LATROBE, PA., U. S. A.
MANUFACTURERS OF SUPERIOR CEMENTED CARBIDES AND CUTTING TOOLS THAT INCREASE PRODUCTION

This advertisement appears in: American Machinist, 8/26/48; Iron Age, 8/5/48; Machinery, 8/48; and Steel, 8/16/48.

photo 8

If you want FREEDOM...
from Unreliable Tooling
from Cheap Money
USE
KENNAMETAL
DEMAND
GOLD COIN STANDARD
Unreliable tools—like cheap money—do not give full value, regardless of their price. The loss due to their unsoundness extends far beyond their own cost—lost man hours, excessive machine downtime, wasted materials.
Kennametal Tooling gives you:
FREEDOM to plan a production schedule and maintain it—getting the greatest benefits from skilled men and good machines.
FREEDOM to machine iron castings having hard, burned, or sandy spots, at high speed—thus saving time and materials.
FREEDOM to machine hard steel—up to 501 Brinell—at high speed, without re-annealing and heat treating.
FREEDOM from experimentation—experienced Kennametal tool engineers can recommend the proper tooling for best results on your jobs.
FREEDOM from guesswork—our complete and accurate Catalog makes it easy to order tools for specific jobs.
Cheap money—like unreliable tools—does not give full value. The consequences of cheap money extend far beyond the demoralizing current effects—spiraling prices, exorbitant taxes, financial insecurity. Ultimate loss of personal liberty, and absolute abrogation of the individual's property rights are inevitable.
Cheap money is the result of the American citizen's inability to control the public purse by demanding and receiving gold in exchange for paper money. Return to the Gold Coin Standard gives you:
FREEDOM from excessive taxes and wild spending of your money by government.
FREEDOM from unfair competition subsidized by government loans out of your tax money.
FREEDOM to keep what you earn and spend it as you please.
FREEDOM to save with assurance that your savings are secure.
FREEDOM from economic conditions unfavorable to enterprise and initiative.
FREEDOM to help check the stealthy advance of Socialism, whose deadly weapon is fiat money.
YOU GET MORE from Less Kennametal
Ask our representatives to demonstrate Kennametal . . . the tooling that reduces costs and increases productivity.
KENNAMETAL
SUPERIOR CEMENTED CARBIDES
KENNAMETAL Inc., LATROBE, PA.
YOU GET LESS from More paper money
Ask your Congressman if he is for or against the Reed Bill HR3262. You and other voters must know.
This advertisement appears in American Machinist, 2/20/50; and Machinery, 2/50.

photo 9

IF YOU VALUE FREEDOM
USE DEPENDABLE TOOLS
• MADE BY KENNAMETAL
DEMAND DEPENDABLE MONEY
• REDEEMABLE IN GOLD
It is impossible to "slip one over" on a lathe, milling machine, or planer. A defective tool breaks down—the dependable tool stays on the job. Kennametal—because its structure is inherently strong, free from flaw and defect, insures faster cutting speeds, more production per tool, fewer tool changes, and lower overall tool costs.
You can depend on Kennametal to machine hard steel—up to 501 Brinell—at high speed, without re-annealing and heat treating. You can depend on it to machine iron castings—hard, burned, and sandy—at faster rates, saving time and materials.
With Kennametal tooling you have freedom to plan a schedule and maintain it—obtaining higher productivity from powerful machines and skilled operators, thus reducing unit costs and adding value to the production dollar.
Your profit is made at the point of the Kennametal cutting tool.
The vigilance of the American public wavered in 1933—and government "slipped one over". The gold coin standard was abandoned, and the dollar was devalued 40%.
Since then, the worth of your savings has been undermined—a bond, insurance, money in the bank has lost over half of its purchasing power. You cannot save for the future with assurance that your savings are secure. A manufacturer cannot set aside a reserve sufficient to pay for equipment that will keep him in business.
Fiat money—a "managed" currency—has always been mismanaged. Today's back-breaking taxes, practically unlimited government spending, and the uncertainty of your future are directly due to unsound money.
These conditions are the breeding grounds of Socialism . . . poisonous to enterprise and initiative . . . death-dealing to personal freedom. A redeemable gold coin standard has always been the only basis for sound, dependable money. Its restoration will prevent embezzlement of your savings—will encourage conditions favorable to personal enterprise—will insure human freedom.
YOU GET MORE from Less Kennametal
Ask our representatives to demonstrate Kennametal . . . the tooling that reduces costs and increases productivity.
KENNAMETAL
SUPERIOR CEMENTED CARBIDES
KENNAMETAL Inc., LATROBE, PA.
YOU GET LESS from More paper money
Ask your Congressman if he is for or against the Reed Bill HR3262. You and other voters must know.
This advertisement appears in American Machinist, 5/29/50; Machinery, 6/50; and Steel, 6/5/50.
PRINTED IN U.S.A.

photo 10

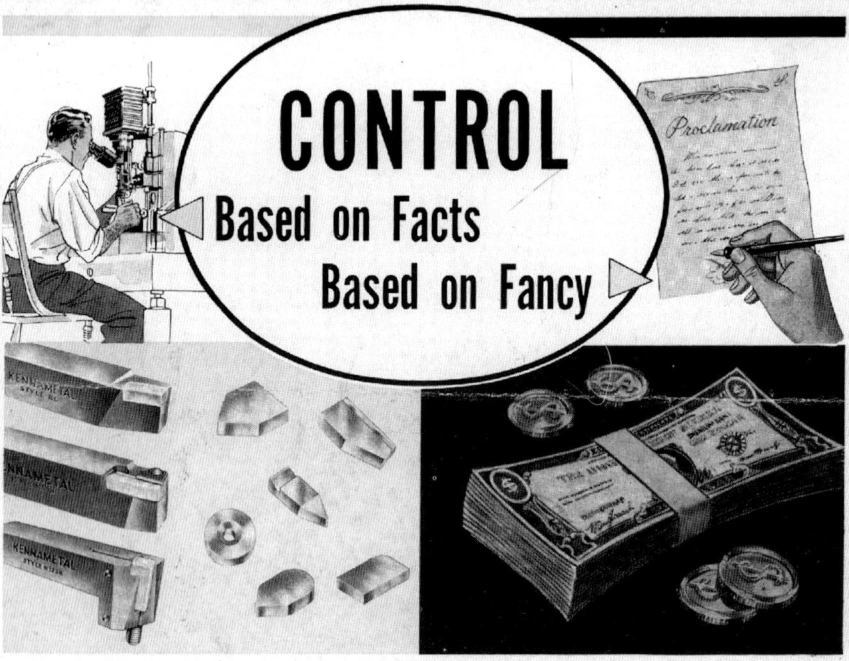

Kennametal is controlled in conformity with precision methods that time and experience have proved to be the best for producing cemented carbides of consistent worth.

Our U.S. currency has, for 15 years, been under arbitrary controls set by official decree in violation of traditional experience with sound money systems.

The controls of Kennametal are exacting and continuous to assure that: basic ingredients are pure; carbides true and of correct particle size; compositions accurately blended; blanks pressed compactly; and sintering processes free from contamination.

Currency control, as now in vogue, is illogical and unscientific. Since anchorage to gold was removed by edict, irredeemable paper certificates have been freely issued. They are merely vague promises to pay amounts not clearly defined—symbols of debt, unsupported by adequate resources.

The rigorous control of Kennametal is an asset. It results in the production of more carbides, yet their value as cost-saving materials is enhanced and maintained. Durability permits a satisfactory job to be done with fewer "units."

The lax control of currency is a liability. Money is no longer a fixed measure for present or future evaluation, a reliable medium of exchange, nor a check on the public purse by citizens. More dollars are in circulation, but their purchasing value has been greatly reduced. Cheap money always brings high prices—because more "units" are required for a given job.

To offset dollar rises in costs during inflation or to safeguard profit margins in times of deflation, you can improve the efficiency of plant operations and increase production by a more widespread use of Kennametal.

To effect correction of deranged economic conditions, you can urge the enactment of legislation that will bring back a stabilized monetary system—the redeemable Gold Standard.

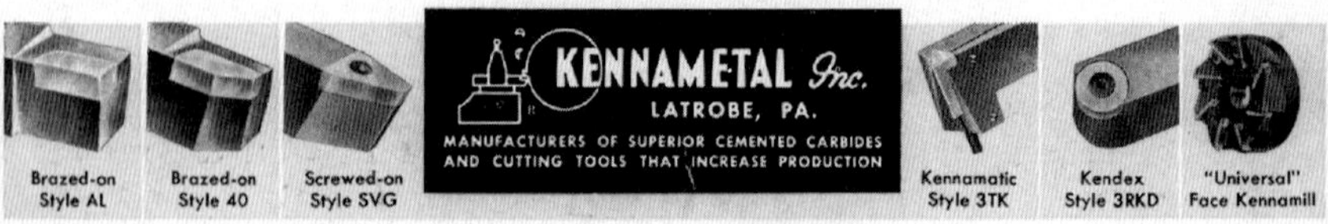

Iron Age, March 10, 1949
Steel, March 21, 1949
American Machinist, March 24, 1949
Machinery, March, 1949
Tool Engineer, March 1949

photo 11

This advertisement appears in Modern Machine Shop, 4/51

PRINTED IN U.S.A.

photo 12

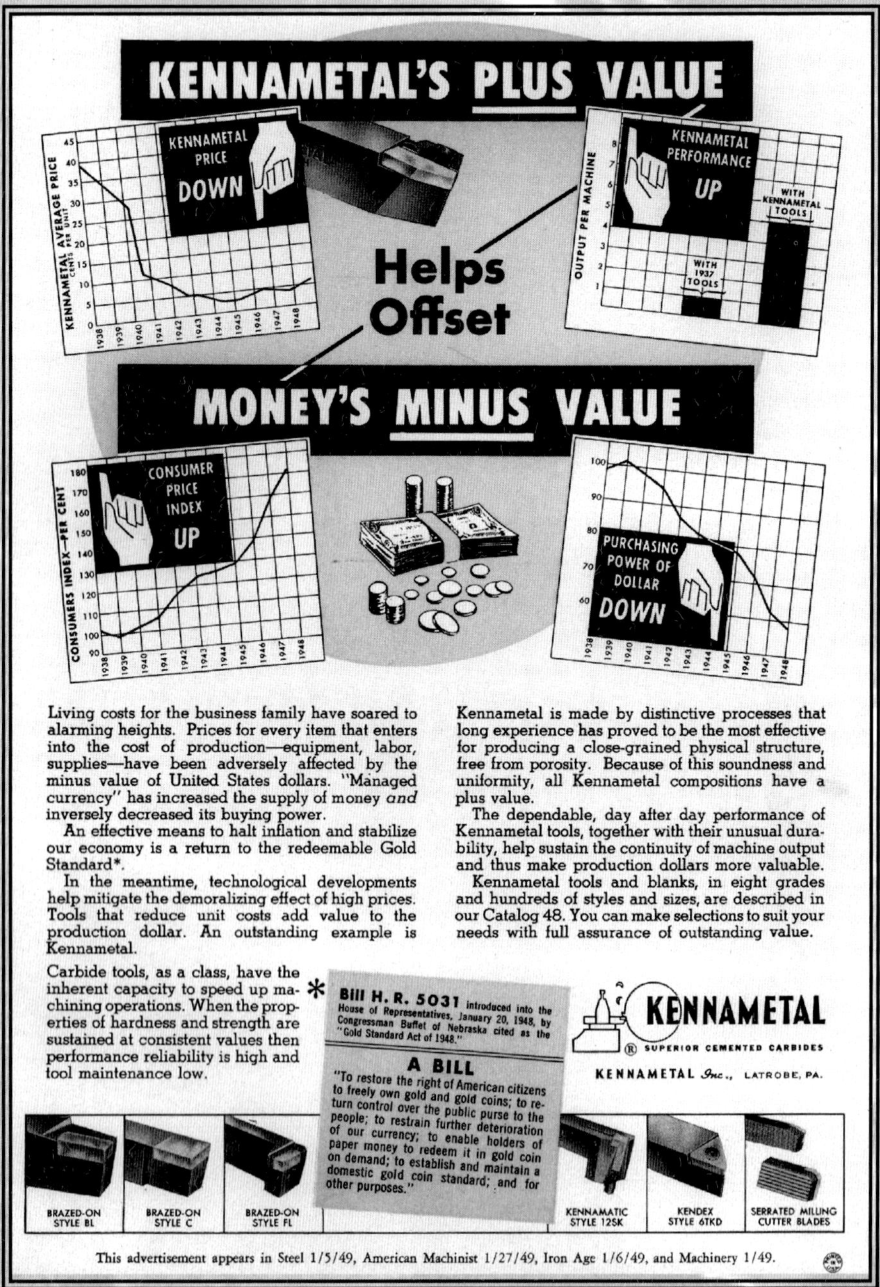
KENNAMETAL'S PLUS VALUE
KENNAMETAL PRICE DOWN
KENNAMETAL AVERAGE PRICE CENTS PER UNIT
KENNAMETAL PERFORMANCE UP
OUTPUT PER MACHINE
WITH 1937 TOOLS
WITH KENNAMETAL TOOLS
Helps Offset
MONEY'S MINUS VALUE
CONSUMER PRICE INDEX UP
CONSUMERS INDEX—PER CENT
PURCHASING POWER OF DOLLAR DOWN
Living costs for the business family have soared to alarming heights. Prices for every item that enters into the cost of production—equipment, labor, supplies—have been adversely affected by the minus value of United States dollars. "Managed currency" has increased the supply of money *and* inversely decreased its buying power.
An effective means to halt inflation and stabilize our economy is a return to the redeemable Gold Standard*.
In the meantime, technological developments help mitigate the demoralizing effect of high prices. Tools that reduce unit costs add value to the production dollar. An outstanding example is Kennametal.
Carbide tools, as a class, have the inherent capacity to speed up machining operations. When the properties of hardness and strength are sustained at consistent values then performance reliability is high and tool maintenance low.
Kennametal is made by distinctive processes that long experience has proved to be the most effective for producing a close-grained physical structure, free from porosity. Because of this soundness and uniformity, all Kennametal compositions have a plus value.
The dependable, day after day performance of Kennametal tools, together with their unusual durability, help sustain the continuity of machine output and thus make production dollars more valuable.
Kennametal tools and blanks, in eight grades and hundreds of styles and sizes, are described in our Catalog 48. You can make selections to suit your needs with full assurance of outstanding value.
* Bill H. R. 5031 introduced into the House of Representatives, January 20, 1948, by Congressman Buffet of Nebraska cited as the "Gold Standard Act of 1948."
A BILL
"To restore the right of American citizens to freely own gold and gold coins; to return control over the public purse to the people; to restrain further deterioration of our currency; to enable holders of paper money to redeem it in gold coin on demand; to establish and maintain a domestic gold coin standard; and for other purposes."
KENNAMETAL
SUPERIOR CEMENTED CARBIDES
KENNAMETAL Inc., LATROBE, PA.
BRAZED-ON STYLE BL
BRAZED-ON STYLE C
BRAZED-ON STYLE FL
KENNAMATIC STYLE 12SK
KENDEX STYLE 6TKD
SERRATED MILLING CUTTER BLADES
This advertisement appears in Steel 1/5/49, American Machinist 1/27/49, Iron Age 1/6/49, and Machinery 1/49.

photo 13

Call the FIREMAN

$100

FREEDOM *is on fire*

The fires of inflation have consumed 60% of the purchasing power of the dollar since 1933, when the government abrogated the people's right to redeem paper money for gold coin.

American industry has been fighting a game but losing battle to overcome the effects of inflation—through increased productivity. Kennametal is an outstanding example—a hard cemented carbide material that multiplies output in metal-cutting plants, cuts and drills coal and other minerals faster with less effort; as a wear-resistant greatly increases the durability of production machines.

The hungry fires of inflation are consuming the benefits of greater productivity . . . the earnings of the industrious . . . the savings of the thrifty . . . worse yet, the incentive of inventor and investor. For enterprise flourishes only when risk can be calculated—and calculation is impossible when the slide rule, money, is unreliable.

It is time to call in the Fireman—the Gold Coin Standard★—to quench the flames of inflation which are fed by the straw of fiat money and fanned by the wind of extravagant government spending. The Gold Coin Standard . . . giving the right to any holder of currency to exchange it for gold when he is displeased with government policy . . . can halt inflation before its flames have gutted our money system, and burned to ashes our freedom.

The return of sound money will encourage American industry, of which Kennametal Inc. is a key enterprise, to achieve ever-increasing productivity—creating greatest material benefits for the individual in a free economy.

★ **WHAT YOU CAN DO ABOUT THE GOLD STANDARD**

Ask your Senators and Congressman if they wish to help restore the Gold Standard with sound money redeemable in gold coin on demand. Write to The Gold Standard League, Latrobe, Pennsylvania for further information. The League is a voluntary association of American citizens joined together to prevent collapse of our monetary system.

First of a Series

KENNAMETAL *Inc.*®
Latrobe, Pa.

WORLD'S LARGEST Independent Manufacturer Whose Facilities are Devoted Exclusively to Processing and Application of CEMENTED CARBIDES

This advertisement appears in Wall Street Journal

PRINTED IN U.S.A.

photo 14

The Best way to End INFLATION

This would not be America if a citizen couldn't criticize government . . . or for that matter, business, labor, or his next-door neighbor. Criticism doesn't necessarily impugn motives or principles. Anyone can make an honest mistake . . . . .

It was a mistake for the government to invalidate the gold coin standard in 1933. The consequences have been serious—and if the mistake is not rectified—can be fatal. Since 1933 purchasing power of the dollar has declined 60%. The value of savings, insurances, pensions have depreciated correspondingly. Government spending has piled up huge public debts. Taxes are drying up earnings and reserves.

These effects have created a chasm between government and business which is foolish and futile . . . the objective of both being the same—to provide better living standards for U.S. citizens.

Business has contributed to this objective through technological advancements, among which Kennametal is an outstanding example. Kennametal, as a tool material, has multiplied the productivity potential of metal-cutting industries, mines, quarries, etc. Yet the benefits of such productivity are being offset by depreciating currency.

It's time for Government and Business to work together. Leaders in government can quickly stop the fall of money by re-establishing the Gold Coin Standard★ . . . which, teamed with the rise in industrial productivity, will bring greater and greater benefits to all our people.

★ WHAT YOU CAN DO ABOUT THE GOLD STANDARD

Ask your Senators and Congressman if they wish to help restore the Gold Standard with sound money redeemable in gold coin on demand. Write to The Gold Standard League, Latrobe, Pennsylvania for further information. The League is a voluntary association of American citizens joined together to prevent collapse of our monetary system.

Number 3 of a Series

KENNAMETAL *Inc.*®

Latrobe, Pa.

WORLD'S LARGEST Independent Manufacturer Whose Facilities are Devoted Exclusively to Processing and Application of CEMENTED CARBIDES

This advertisement appears in Wall Street Journal

PRINTED IN U.S.A.

photo 15

This CONTROL is needed in a FREE ECONOMY

When the power to control public money is taken from the hands of the people, its purchasing value inevitably becomes less and less. It has always been so. Since 1933, when the government abrogated the people's right to exchange paper money for gold, the value of the dollar has constantly descended.

The incentive to save is gone . . . expansion of production facilities is hampered. Kennametal Inc. is a case in point. We make hard cemented carbide tool materials which can triple production in metal-cutting and other vital industries. This is the type of industrial product that keeps America far ahead in technological advancement.

Investors have always before contributed much to the realization of American enterprise. Today, however, they are handicapped by high taxes, and hampered by all the uncertainties that go hand-in-hand with unsound money.

The public must again be given control of the government's purse strings. We must return to the Gold Coin Standard★ . . . which gives the people the right to express lack of confidence in government policy, if necessary, by redeeming their currency for gold.

When this control has been restored to the people—wasteful government spending will be stopped—and American industry, of which Kennametal Inc. is a key enterprise, will be able to plan and produce with the vitality that exists only in a free economy.

Number 5 of a Series

★ WHAT YOU CAN DO ABOUT THE GOLD STANDARD

Ask your Senators and Congressman if they wish to help restore the Gold Standard with sound money redeemable in gold coin on demand. Write to The Gold Standard League, Latrobe, Pennsylvania for further information. The League is a voluntary association of American citizens joined together to prevent collapse of our monetary system.

KENNAMETAL Inc.®
Latrobe, Pa.

WORLD'S LARGEST Independent Manufacturer Whose Facilities are Devoted Exclusively to Processing and Application of CEMENTED CARBIDES

This advertisement appears in Wall Street Journal

PRINTED IN U.S.A.

photo 16

It's a HELL of a Way to HAUL A LOAD

Business is asked to increase productivity—but is seriously hampered by unstable, depreciating currency. Taxes eat up earnings, adequate reserves cannot be set aside for plant improvement and technical research—and the value of these insufficient reserves continues to shrink as inflation rolls on.

Kennametal Inc., is typical as a business—but unique in its production. We manufacture hard cemented carbide materials that other industries use to increase their productivity: For tools that triple metal-cutting output, and greatly speed extraction of coal and other minerals; wear-parts that improve the durability of machinery; gas turbine parts that extend the life and better the performance of aircraft jet engines.

These products haul American industry along the road to progress—but unsound money pulls in the opposite direction.

The way to get money back into the right harness, pulling with free enterprise, is to restore the Gold Coin Standard★. It puts control of the public purse into the hands of the people—since any holder of currency may redeem it for gold if he is displeased with government policy. And—fiat money—fundamental cause of inflation, is the first government policy that needs to be retired to pasture.

When this is done all manufacturers, including Kennametal Inc., will be able to achieve greater productivity—which is the only road America can travel to arrive at better living standards for all of our people.

Number 7 of a Series

★ **WHAT YOU CAN DO ABOUT THE GOLD STANDARD**

Ask your Senators and Congressman if they wish to help restore the Gold Standard with sound money redeemable in gold coin on demand. Write to The Gold Standard League, Latrobe, Pennsylvania for further information. The League is a voluntary association of American citizens joined together to prevent collapse of our monetary system.

KENNAMETAL Inc.®
Latrobe, Pa.

WORLD'S LARGEST Independent Manufacturer Whose Facilities are Devoted Exclusively to Processing and Application of CEMENTED CARBIDES

This advertisement appears in Wall Street Journal

PRINTED IN U.S.A.

photo 17

Kentanium is our new and exclusive development—a titanium alloy that is ideally suited for gas turbine parts because it withstands high temperature and other conditions that destroy conventional alloys. Kentanium, when adopted, can greatly improve the performance and increase the service life of jet plane engines—yet it contains neither of the critical materials, tungsten and cobalt. Kentanium is available to fight Communism.

Sound money is another "secret" weapon—but it is not available. Instead the U.S. economy is inflicted with a pseudo-sound, fiat currency that is the underlying cause of inflation. Such unsound money is a weapon of Communism—and we are using it against ourselves. Remember—Lenin is reported to have said that the surest way to overturn an existing social order is to debauch the currency.

Sound money is sorely needed in the fight against Communism . . . and the only sound money system that has ever been successful is the Gold Coin Standard★. It stabilizes the value of money . . . prevents issuance of fiat currency . . . and gives the individual close control over government policy since he can redeem his currency for gold coin whenever such policy is inimical to preservation of individual rights and liberty.

Return to sound money will provide the incentive that spurs inventors and investors to produce industrial advancements—such as Kennametal and its sister product Kentanium—which keep America's productivity far in front of Communism.

★ WHAT YOU CAN DO ABOUT THE GOLD STANDARD

Ask your Senators and Congressman if they wish to help restore the Gold Standard with sound money redeemable in gold coin on demand. Write to The Gold Standard League, Latrobe, Pennsylvania for further information. The League is a voluntary association of American citizens joined together to prevent collapse of our monetary system.

Number 9 of a Series

KENNAMETAL Inc.®
Latrobe, Pa.

WORLD'S LARGEST Independent Manufacturer Whose Facilities are Devoted Exclusively to Processing and Application of CEMENTED CARBIDES

This advertisement appears in Wall Street Journal

PRINTED IN U.S.A.

photo 18

"KENNAMETAL . . .
the super hard tool material—multiplies metal cutting output—speeds up coal and mineral production."

"KENTANIUM . . .
the titanium alloy, containing no tungsten or cobalt, greatly extends service life of aircraft gas turbines."

"GOLD COIN STANDARD . . .
stops inflation, controls government spending, stabilizes value of currency, savings and investments."

Why Doesn't Someone Tell Me These Things?

Kennametal Inc. makes vital materials for America's peacetime or wartime production: Kennametal—super-hard cemented carbide that multiplies production in metal-cutting and other industries; and Kentanium—used for gas turbine parts, enabling jet plane engines to operate far longer at higher temperature.

We are sometimes surprised to find a few production men who don't know about the advantages of Kennametal—and a few military men who don't know about Kentanium and how we make it without the use of the critical materials, tungsten and cobalt.

We are even more surprised when these and other men seem wholly unaware of the importance of a Gold Coin Standard★ . . . and why its absence is the basic reason for reckless government spending and accelerating inflation.

To stop inflation—control of the public purse must be returned to the public. The Gold Coin Standard . . . the right to convert paper money into gold coin . . . abrogated in 1933 . . . will end irresponsible issue of fiat currency, curb reckless government spending, prevent the government's use of its liabilities as collateral for the issuance of printing paper money.

Fortunately—practically all key men know how Kennametal and Kentanium can contribute to industrial productivity. Unfortunately, far too few realize how fiat currency dilutes the benefits of greater productivity and gradually destroys individual freedom.

Number 11 of a Series

★ **WHAT YOU CAN DO ABOUT THE GOLD STANDARD**

Ask your Senators and Congressman if they wish to help restore the Gold Standard with sound money redeemable in gold coin on demand. Write to The Gold Standard League, Latrobe, Pennsylvania, for further information. The League is a voluntary association of American citizens joined together to prevent collapse of our monetary system.

KENNAMETAL® Inc.
Latrobe, Pa.

WORLD'S LARGEST Independent Manufacturer Whose Facilities are Devoted Exclusively to Processing and Application of CEMENTED CARBIDES

This advertisement appears in Wall Street Journal

PRINTED IN U.S.A.

photo 19

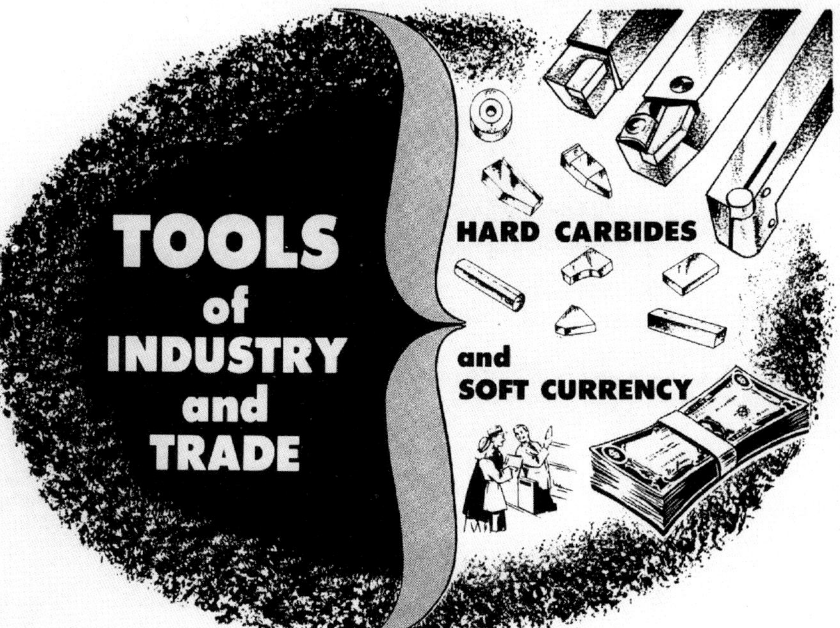

MONEY, certified as to weight and fineness by our Federal Government, and Kennametal Tools, made by Kennametal Inc.—a private concern at Latrobe, Pa.—are both tools of present and potential value to a free America.

How is sound money a necessary tool for free people? It facilitates honest exchange of goods and services between persons. Thus it is used as a measuring tool. How well it serves its purpose depends upon the degree of certainty which persons may place upon its present and future value.

Kennametal Tool Blanks and Kennametal Tools merit confidence as to their value. They facilitate daily production in metal-working shops, in mines, and in construction work, enabling the workers to do their work effectively, thus helping maintain high standards of living in times of peace and providing weapons for our defense in times of war. Durability, hardness, and utility are embodied in Kennametal products.

Money will serve its necessary purposes, inspiring thrift, lending for worth-while enterprise, and protecting the real value of savings accounts, life insurance, and customary forms of saving, only when uncertainty is removed by stabilizing our currency, as proposed in a bill now pending before Congress*. A deteriorating, non-redeemable money robs all who earn and save.

There is no uncertainty about Kennametal. It is not a mere fiat certificate of value; it has intrinsic worth—lasting merit—as valuable 10 years hence as now—one piece equally as good as another.

This uniformly excellent tool material is obtainable "on demand" at our plant at Latrobe, Pa., or any of our branches in industrial centers of the United States. It is truly the "All American Carbide". From our new Catalog 48 you can order the tool tips and complete tools you need, with assurance that full value will always be realized.

Gold is the Tool that Shapes World Security

"I wonder what the Vintners buy
One half so precious as the Goods they sell."
Rubaiyat of Omar Khayyam

* **Bill H. R. 5031** introduced into the House of Representatives, January 20, 1948, by Congressman Buffet of Nebraska cited as the "Gold Standard Act of 1948."

A BILL

"To restore the right of American citizens to freely own gold and gold coins; to return control over the public purse to the people; to restrain further deterioration of our currency; to enable holders of paper money to redeem it in gold coin on demand; to establish and maintain a domestic gold coin standard; and for other purposes."

® **KENNAMETAL**
SUPERIOR CEMENTED CARBIDES
KENNAMETAL *Inc.*, LATROBE, PA.

This advertisement appears in: Pittsburgh Post-Gazette and Latrobe Bulletin, 8/10/48.

photo 20

It seems to me...

by Philip M. McKenna

President, Kennametal Inc., Latrobe, Pa.

How long can we remain half free and half socialist?

When a government outlaws the right of individual ownership of gold, it takes the first step . . . perhaps the most important step . . . toward complete control of the nation.

Hitler proved this truism when he took away from the Germans the right of citizens to use gold, and then went on to enslave the nation. Mussolini repeated it in Italy, with complete subservience of Italians to his totalitarian domination.

Back in 1933, our Government took us off the Gold Standard. U. S. Citizens were forbidden the right to own gold. We lost the power to demand gold in exchange for our dollars, and with it, the power to control the Governmental purse strings. Thus, we lost a part of our freedom and invited socialism.

It seems to me that we can't live too long as a half-free, half-socialist nation. Already the government takes one-third of our income in taxes, and, besides, has given us a 50¢ dollar through inflation brought about by continuous deficit spending. It seems to me that socialism will overwhelm us . . . that is, unless we re-establish our independence with the protection of the Gold Coin Standard.

The Gold Coin Standard will help us in other ways. It will re-establish, for example, a standard of value to work with, to plan with, to build on.

The standard will also make it possible for industry to pass along to buyers of goods in the form of lower prices, all savings resulting from inventions,† developments and production improvements, such as, for example, those made by Kennametal.*

Don't you think this deserves some extra thought and discussion? I'll be glad to hear from you . . . about the Gold Coin Standard, as well as about Kennametal and what this hard, man-made metal can do for America. KENNAMETAL INC., Latrobe, Pennsylvania.

†The invention of Kennametal made possible the high speed machining of steel and steel alloys. Kennametal's latest development — Grade K21 — is another step to increase production, to bring additional savings to the metalworking industry . . . savings that could be passed on to every buyer of goods if we were moving along with a Gold Coin Standard.

*Kennametal is the registered trademark of a series of hard carbide alloys of tungsten, tungsten-titanium and tantalum, for tooling in the metalworking, mining and woodworking industries, and for wear parts in machines and processing equipment.

7294

One of a series of advertisements in the public interest

MINING, METAL AND WOODWORKING TOOLS

WEAR AND HEAT-RESISTANT PARTS

INDUSTRY AND KENNAMETAL

...Partners in Progress

ABRASION, CORROSION-RESISTANT PARTS

PERCUSSION AND IMPACT PARTS

A-7294

This advertisement is scheduled to appear in:
The Freeman

photo 21

How To Make GOOD MONEY!

EVERY WORKER wants to make money —to assure a comfortable living for today, and to provide a nest egg for tomorrow, in the form of savings, insurance, or pensions.

Money is plentiful today; but cheap. Its purchasing power has been greatly depreciated.

How did this come about? The Gold Reserve Act was passed by Congress in 1934, which removed gold coins from circulation, and arbitrarily raised the price of gold from $20.00 an ounce to $35.00. This enabled more paper dollars, of less value in gold, to be printed and put into circulation.

What has been the effect? Daniel Webster once said, "Of all the contrivances for cheating the laboring classes of mankind, none has been more effective than that which deludes them with paper money."

Since 1934 there has been a continual and relentless rise in the cost of living. The United States dollar has shrunk in value to 37¢. A daily wage of $10.00 is required to buy what $3.70 would buy 15 years ago. A monthly pension of $100.00 has dwindled to $37.00 in buying power. A $1000.00 insurance policy taken out in 1934 will provide only $370.00 in value for today's beneficiary. Thus depreciated currency is a basic cause of price rises, and wage increases are required to offset them.

Where will this vicious spiral end? Innumerable historic instances have proved that when governments "manage" currency to finance huge public debts, and thereby deny citizens the right to use money of intrinsic value, other liberties of free peoples are threatened.

The founder and great apostle of Bolshevism, Lenin, declared and demonstrated that of all the methods to overthrow a free economy and bring about communism, there is none so stealthy in its approach, and so certain of success as to print irredeemable paper money.

"Best tool of tyrants," Lenin said
"Debauch their money, then step in,
Coordination's in the head;
Disrupt their ways, make it a sin
To bargain free. When terror rules,
Our agents rise, control these fools."

Whenever economic chaos comes, those who feel it most are always the common people, the wage earners, those who depend upon what they have "laid by for a rainy day." This was true in ancient and medieval countries, as well as in Russia, France, Italy, and Germany of more recent times.

Do we want chaotic conditions in our Country? How can we prevent them? The most trustworthy money system ever devised is the convertible Gold Standard. A bill has been introduced into Congress, HR 5031, which is intended "To restore the right of American citizens to freely own gold and gold coins; to return control over the public purse to the people; to restrain further deterioration of our currency; to enable holders of paper money to redeem it in gold on demand . . ."

Enactment of this bill, which is really anti-communistic, will have a stabilizing influence on our economy, will enable the individual to again know with certainty the worth of his earnings and SAVINGS, and permit business concerns to plan ahead so that workers can make GOOD money.

KENNAMETAL Inc.
LATROBE, PA.

MANUFACTURERS OF SUPERIOR CEMENTED CARBIDE METAL-CUTTING AND MINING TOOLS

photo 22

IS YOUR MONEY AS GOOD AS GOLD?

IF YOU THINK SO...

Just Try to Swap It!

The redeemable Gold Standard was cancelled by your government in 1933 so that it could "manage" money—*your* money. At the same time, your government cheapened money—*your* money—by increasing the price of gold.

What happened after that should never have happened to a hard-working, thrifty people. But it did happen—and it is costing *you* money. And it will cost you more money—unless you do something about it.

Prices are up. How well you know it! The **paper dollar** is worth only about **52 cents** . . . in value . . . compared to its worth 10 years ago.

Also—you have been deprived of the right to own gold coin. And **this right** has always—in the world's history—been the **greatest safeguard of personal liberty.**

When you own gold—or paper certificates that can be freely redeemed in gold—you can save with assurance and plan for the future. For—in good times or bad—the world over—money is as good as gold—only when it is freely convertible to gold. *You do not have that kind of money.*

What can you do about it? Go into action—write your Congressman, urging him to support the Gold Standard bill now before the House of Representatives—H. R. Bill 3262.

Write to us for a copy of the bill. We will send it, and other very interesting material on the Gold Standard, free of charge.

Philip M. McKenna
National Chairman
Gold Standard League
One Lloyd Avenue, Latrobe, Pa.

photo 23

WHAT IS YOUR DOLLAR WORTH ?

IF YOU WANT TO LEARN THE TRUTH

Go to your bank . . . and try to have your currency made good in Gold

Your banker will be glad to exchange your paper dollar for another paper dollar . . . but ask for gold—and all you'll get will be a lifted eyebrow. For your banker, like you, is forbidden, by law, to possess gold coin.

In 1933—The United States government relinquished the Gold Standard—and arbitrarily raised the price of gold. Was it **high financing**—that wouldn't affect the "average" person?

We don't have to tell you the answer—you are now **paying the bill.** When the government increased the price of gold—the **value** of the dollar in gold **decreased.** In time the **value** of food, clothing, and shelter **increased**—so it takes more dollars to buy them. This was a fundamental reason for higher prices.

But—why doesn't the government permit you to own gold? Because it wishes to manage the economy and lives of the American people.

There is more gold stored in Fort Knox—over $24,000,000,000.00 worth of it—than has ever been held by any other nation in world history.

Printing-press money has never been permanent.

Gold has a permanent value—in good times and bad—throughout the world.

The right to own gold is necessary to individual security and personal liberty.

What can you do about it? Do this, and do it now. Write your Congressman—and tell your friends to write—urging him to support the Gold Standard act now before the House of Representatives—H. R. Bill 3262. And—write us for further particulars and suggestions.

Philip M. McKenna
National Chairman
Gold Standard League
One Lloyd Avenue, Latrobe, Pa.

photo 24

Did our Government Play into the Communists' Hands When It Took Your Gold . . . ?

NICOLAI LENIN
First President of U.S.S.R.

Nicolai Lenin, the first President of Communist Russia, is reported to have declared that the surest way to overturn the existing social order is to **debauch the currency** . . . and Lenin's prime objective in life was, like Stalin's today, the overthrow of every capitalistic economy in the world. The founder of Soviet Russia, had he still been alive, would have laughed outright when our government in 1933 called in all outstanding gold and deprived American cltizens of the right to possess it.

A confused money system guarantees a confused economy . . . we see it everywhere today, in **high prices**, in **business uncertainty**, in **exorbitant taxes**, in man's **inability to plan a secure future** for himself and his family. Yet the government responsible for all this holds most of the world's gold bullion—more than 24 billion dollars' worth, in its vaults at Fort Knox. It is time that American citizens insisted on the restoration of their **proper right** to redeem their paper currency for **honest, worthwhile gold.**

What can you do about it? Go into action—write your Congressman, urging him to support the Gold Standard bill now before the House of Representatives—H. R. Bill 3262.

Write to us for a copy of the bill. We will send it, and other very interesting material on the Gold Standard, free of charge.

Philip M. McKenna
National Chairman
Gold Standard League
One Lloyd Avenue, Latrobe, Pa.

photo 25

READ THE FINE PRINT ON THESE CONTRACTS

Your Right to Own Gold Has Been Violated

Do you know that every piece of paper money you own or ever did own constitutes a contract, by which your government has agreed to do certain things, in return for your willingness to accept paper instead of "hard cash?"

Once you could exchange any type of money which you possessed for gold or silver. The government defaulted on that promise sixteen years ago, insofar as gold payments are concerned, and forced you to return to the government all gold or gold certificates which you possessed.

Read the promise made on a Federal Reserve note which was current in 1932. Read in contrast the **meaningless promise made on that note today.** An honest currency is fundamental to honest government. **A dishonest money** system is undermining American prosperity, stripping your earnings of their value, clouding your future with doubt and uncertainty.

What can you do about it? Go into action—write your Congressman, urging him to support the Gold Standard bill now before the House of Representatives—H. R. Bill 3262.

Write to us for a copy of the bill. We will send it, and other very interesting material on the Gold Standard, free of charge.

Philip M. McKenna
National Chairman
Gold Standard League
One Lloyd Avenue, Latrobe, Pa.

photo 26

IF YOU ARE AN AMERICAN . . .

YOU CAN'T TAKE IT WITH YOU

You . . . an American citizen . . . cannot redeem paper money for gold. No matter how hard you work . . . or how high your pay—The United States government will not permit you to purchase or possess gold coin.

But—any **foreign nation** may **sell** its services or products to us . . . demand gold (your gold) from our government—and take it away.

Why are you **discriminated** against? It's a fair question, and it deserves a fair reply.

Plenty of Gold Available

Our government has the greatest amount of gold ever accumulated in the world's history. More than $24,000,000,000.00 in gold is stored at Fort Knox. That's about *double* the amount held by all the other nations of the world.

Your Right to Own Gold

A redeemable currency—which means that you and every other American citizen has the right to redeem paper money for gold coin—is the most practical and reliable measure of value ever devised.

It provides assurance that **earnings, savings, insurance policies,** and **other investments** will have permanent value. It takes control of *your* purse away from politics and puts it back into your own hands. That's where it should be.

What can you do about it? Just this—write your Congressman, urging him to support the Gold Standard bill now before the House of Representatives—H. R. Bill 3262.

Write to us for a copy of the bill. We will send it and other pertinent, interesting material on the Gold Standard, free of charge.

Philip M. McKenna
National Chairman
Gold Standard League
One Lloyd Avenue, Latrobe, Pa.

photo 27

Hon. Daniel A. Reed, N.Y.

"An irredeemable currency system is as ruthless in its devastating effects as the invasion of an army."

An address before the Gold Standard League Convention in Washington, D.C., on May 5, 1952

photo 28

Senator Francis Case, South Dakota, addressing the Gold Standard League, Washington, D.C., May 5, 1952

"Restore the right to citizens to own gold and gold coins!"

photo 29

photo 30

From the left to the right: Percy Greaves Jr. (American Party candidate for the U.S. in 1980), Fred G. Clark (founded Crusaders Against Prohibition in 1929), Philip M. McKenna, Frank Chodorov (one of the founders of the Intercollegiate Studies Institute), and Paul Bakewell, Jr. (his affiliation is unknown).

Rev. Armand Jean Baldwin, St. Vincent College and Philip M. McKenna - Washington, D.C., May 5, 1952

"Morality and honest money go hand in hand."

photo 31

Rev. Armand Jean Baldwin was a professor of Political Science at Saint Vincent College from 1939 to 1979. From 1949 to 1962, Rev. Baldwin was the chair of the Economics Department, and from 1962 to 1972, he was the chair of the Political Science and Economics Departments.

photo 32

Press Conference December 1, 1953. Standing is Dr. Glenn Olin Saxon, professor of Economics at Yale University 1931 to 1961. The person furthest to the right is Henry S. Hazlett, literary editor at *The Nation*, top editorialist at the *New York Times*, and weekly columnist at *Newsweek*.

photo 33

Philip showing gold coin to Dr. Walter Spahr (center), chair of Economics at NYU from 1928 to 1956, and H.J. Stuhlmiller, president of States Savings Bank in Iowa.

photo 34

Philip M. McKenna and Senator Harry Byrd of Virginia at the Virginia Nurserymen's Association Meeting, January 30, 1950

photo 35

Donald C. McKenna (left), Philip's brother, chairman of the Board of Kennametal Inc., and Alex G. McKenna, Philip's first cousin and President and CEO of Kennametal Inc., May 1, 1970.

photo 36

Philip M. McKenna on the shop floor at Kennametal Inc., January 30, 1953.

photo 37

Philip M. McKenna, January 30, 1953.

Index

Information located in footnotes is indicated by n. References to photographs are indicated by Photo.